A GUIDE TO
BRITISH ARMY
BADGES
–
A GALLERY OF
INFANTRY OF THE LINE
RARITIES
1751 TO 1881

A GUIDE TO BRITISH ARMY BADGES

—

A GALLERY OF INFANTRY OF THE LINE RARITIES 1751 TO 1881

The Naval & Military Press

© Ray Westlake. 2022

For Alan Seymour,
a good friend for more than thirty-five years

Published by

The Naval & Military Press Ltd
Unit 5 Riverside
Bellbrook Industrial Estate
Uckfield, East Sussex
TN22 1QQ
England

Tel: +44 (0) 1825 749494

www.naval-military-press.com

CONTENTS

ACKNOWLEDGEMENTS viii

INTRODUCTION ix

INFANTRY REGIMENTS OF THE LINE 1

APPENDIX 171

BIBLIOGRAPHY 174

ACKNOWLEDGEMENTS

This book would not have been possible without the generosity of the following in allowing me to use images from their catalogues, collections and sales lists: Alan Seymour, the Anne SK Brown Military Collection, Bosley's Military Auctions, Blues Military Collectables, Coldstream Military Antiques, Cultman Collectables, Les Martin, Noble Numismatics, Regimental Badges, The Military Campaign and Thomas Del Mar Ltd. Also to my guide in all things, my wife Claire.

INTRODUCTION

This 'Guide' is not intended to be a catalogue of badges, but simply an opportunity to record and illustrate some of the rarest items yet noted—shako and shoulder-belt plates worn by the Georgians; the glengarry badges, waist-belt clasps and helmet plates of the Victorians. The scope is 1751 to 1881. The subjects, the 109 numbered regiments of foot that in 1881 went to form the regular battalions of the British Army's new infantry—the so called 'Territorial' or 'County' regiments created by Secretary of State for War, Hugh Childers's Army reforms. Some 300 images have been included.

INFANTRY REGIMENTS OF THE LINE

1st or the Royal Scots Regiment

1 From LC Leask and HM McCance's 1914 regimental history, impressions of two Colours: that of a lieutenant-Colonel of 1680 (top), and another of a First Captain of 1687 (bottom). Both feature a crowned thistle above a sprig of leaves within a circle inscribed with the motto *Nemo me impune lacessit* (No one provokes me with impunity), which has been placed upon a white saltire on a blue background.

2 Colour plate from the Leask and McCance history showing a grenadier company private of 1751 (left) and another of the same rank from a battalion company for the year 1742 (right). For the grenadier, the cap is a good representation of that described in a warrant of 14 September 1743 concerning dress and badges.

3 The early shoulder-belt plates have been noted as being 'probably' oval, gilt and with the design of the Star of the Order of the Thistle. Certainly, oval plates are being worn by all three men (from left to right a private, drummer and officer) in this colour plate dated 1792 from the Leask and McCance history.

4 From the saleroom of Olympia Auctions, a superb example of an officers' gorget. JC Leask and HM McCance date this item as '1800' (gorgets being abolished in 1830). A crowned 'GR' cypher appears engraved to the front, the sides having matching devices attached comprising thistles within crowned circles engraved with the motto Nemo me impune lacessit (No one provokes me with impunity). A scroll below each reads: 'The Royal'. *(Photo courtesy of Thomas Del Mar Ltd)*

Lieut. Colonel's Colour 1680.

First Captain's Colour 1687.

5 Sketch of the shako plate worn by officers between 1813 and 1816. In gilt, this was the universal shape of plate worn by infantry, the regimental badges displayed in this instance being: the King's Cypher within the Collar of the Order of the Thistle, the Badge of the Order and the Sphinx within a wreath. The title 'The Royal Scots' appears on a three-part scroll. The several components (Star, St Andrew and Cross, Thistle, motto, the Collar and Badge) of the Most Ancient and Most Noble Order of the Thistle had been in use by the regiment from quite early on in its history. Certainly, they had been recorded in an Army List published by Nathan Brooks in October 1684 and noted on Colours four years later. The Royal Cypher dates from 1707 when, according to regimental historians JC Leask and HM McCance, it was obtained as a regimental badge displayed within the Collar.

6 A superb example of the plate worn by officers of the 2nd Battalion on the Albert Shako of 1844 to 1855. In gilt, and what at the time was a universal crowned star, it has a thistle wreath with a scroll inscribed 'Waterloo' across the bottom joint. Within this is a circle inscribed 'The Royal Regiment' and in the centre the regimental number. Above the wreath is the Sphinx over 'Egypt'—authorised as a commemoration of the services of the 2nd Battalion during the campaign of 1801—and above that a scroll carrying the battle honour 'Peninsular'. On the lower point of the star is the figure of St Andrew and Cross, it being the badge of the Order of the Thistle. There are more battle honours on the rays of the star: 'Vittoria', 'Ava', 'Egmontopzee', 'Busaco', 'St Lucia', 'Corunna', 'Nagpore', 'Maheidpore', 'Nive', 'St Sebastian', 'Niagara' and 'Salamanca'. *(Photo courtesy of Thomas Del Mar Ltd)*

7 JC Leask and HM McCance date this officers' shako plate to a grenadier company of the 1st Battalion, 1st Regiment as 1844 to 1854, the authors reminding their readers at the same time that during this period special plates were worn by officers of flank (grenadier and light) companies. In the centre, the flames of a grenade can be seen above a circle inscribed with the title 'Royal Regiment' and enclosing the regimental number. Below the circle is the battle honour 'Peninsular' on a scroll and below that, the Sphinx over 'Egypt'. Thirteen other battle honours appear on the rays of the crowned star.

8 In this detailed colour plate dated 1853 from Leask and McCance's regimental history, we have three main figures: from left to right a grenadier company corporal, a battalion company colour sergeant and an officer from the 1st Battalion's light company. Albert pattern shakos are being worn, the grenadier corporal's having in addition to the numeral '1' on the plate, a grenade. The light company officer also has a distinction in the form of a large gilt bugle on his sword belt below an oblong plate.

9 Worn on the 'French' pattern shako of 1855 to 1861, this plate is in gilt and has the 'VR' cypher within a representation of the Collar of the Order of the Thistle. Above this is 'Royal Regiment' on a scroll and below, the badge of the Order. *(Photo courtesy of Thomas Del Mar Ltd)*

10 From JC Leask and HM McCance's history of the regiment is this sketch of an officers' shako plate for which they give a date of 1854 to 1862. This would be the so-called 'French Pattern' shako, taken into use at the end of the Crimean War and authorised by a Horse Guards circular memorandum dated 16 January 1855. All in gilt, the plate has the regimental number on a black enamelled centre within a pierced Garter.

11 A detailed photograph of Captain St George Gray's Company, 1st Regiment, taken in India in 1870. Clearly visible worn in the round caps is the metal number '1'. *(Photo courtesy of Alan Seymour)*

12 A decorative and short-lived item in use as an officers' plate after the introduction of the home service helmet in 1878 and worn until 1881. St Andrew appears in the centre of the Collar of the Order of the Thistle on a blue enamel background. Above this is the title scroll 'The Royal Scots', and below another inscribed *Nemo me Impune lacessit* (No one provokes me with impunity). *(Photo courtesy of Bosley's Military Auctions)*

13 From the Leask and McCance's history, a sketch of a field officers' belt plate for the period 1842 to 1855. In burnished gilt, the crowned cypher and number were in silver.

14 From the Leask and McCance's history, a sketch of an officers' waist-belt clasp dated 1859 to 1872. The author's description is as follows: 'Dead gilt, circle silver, the letters cut bright on matte background, silver St Andrew on dead gilt matte centre.'

15 From the Leask and McCance's history, a sketch of the other ranks', all-brass, waist-belt clasp for the period 1855 to 1872.

2nd (Queen's Royal) Regiment

16 This sketch of an oval shoulder-belt plate is based on an item noted in 1939 as part of the regimental museum's collection. (*Journal of the Society for Army Historical Research*, Volume 18, No 72). The author, the Rev Percy Sumner, described the plate as being silver, very small and with no hallmark: 'The design is a small crown beaten out, and the letters 'C.R.' cut like a stencil.' The Rev Sumner goes on to describe the item as having a beaded edge, and with two pairs of studs at the back. One of the regiment's mottos, Pristinæ virtutis memor (Mindful of former valour), can be seen across the bottom edge of the plate. An alternative spelling of the first word, however, has been used.

17 In this original watercolour painting by Reginald Augustus Wymer (1849-1835) we see featured a sergeant of the 2nd Regiment wearing the shako of the 1800 to 1812 period. The die-struck brass plate is of the universal type with the Royal Cypher 'GR' surrounded by the Garter and surmounted by a crown. On either side are trophies of flags, weapons and trumpets and below, the crowned Lion of England. An oval shoulder-belt plate is being worn which appears to have a crown over the number '2'. (*Image courtesy of the Anne SK Brown Military Collection, Brown University*)

18 In his valuable book, *(Military) Shoulder-Belt Plates and Buttons* (Gale & Polden, Aldershot 1956), Major HG Parkyn records that the colourful officers' shoulder-belt plate of gilt and silver, blue, green and red enamels illustrated had been adopted in 1830. The central device takes the form of a crowned strap which has been pierced with the motto *Pristinæ Virtutis memor* (Mindful of former valour). Behind the letters is a ground of dark red enamel. In the centre, and in silver against blue, is the regiment's ancient Pascal Lamb badge standing on a field of green which displays the regimental number. A silver wreath of laurel surrounds the strap, at the bottom of which has been placed the figure of a Sphinx above 'Egypt'. For the Peninsular War, a total of eight battle honours appear (four each side) on the wreath: 'Corunna', 'Vittoria', 'Nivelle', 'Peninsula' on the left, 'Vimiera', 'Salamanca', 'Pyrenees' and 'Toulouse' on the right. (*Photo courtesy of The Military Campaign*)

19 The Queen's was second in the British Line and its number, together with its Lamb device, is seen here in the centre of a crowned strap. An officers' item, the plate has the 'GR' cypher (one letter either side) engraved on a plain, polished, silver ground and strangely, no inscription on the strap, although close examination suggests that the expected motto Pristinæ virtutis memor (Mindful of former valour) may have been present at one point. Just below the strap is a delicately engraved sprig of laurel. The usually reliable and comprehensive *(Military) Shoulder-belt Plates and Buttons* by Major HG Parkyn makes no mention of this item.

20 An original watercolour painting by Richard Simkin featuring five members of the regiment in undress uniforms. The artist gives the dates ranging from 1836 to 1880. Four of the men are wearing forage caps with Lamb over '2' badges at the front. The fifth study, that of the private on the far left, has a round cap with only the number '2'. Also seen is a rectangular, brass shoulder-belt plate with a crown above '2'. *(Image courtesy of the Anne SK Brown Military Collection, Brown University)*

21 A fine example of the plate worn by officers on the shako authorised by Horse Guards Circular Memorandum dated 16 January 1855. An eight-pointed, gilt crowned star, the plate displays the regimental Paschal Lamb badge and number in silver on a red ground within a pierced Garter. *(Photo courtesy of Coldstream Military Antiques)*

22 In this photograph of a group of officers, the regiment's Pascal Lamb can be seen worn above the numeral '2' in the forage caps. *(Photo courtesy of Alan Seymour)*

23 An officers' gilt and silver plate worn on what was to become the last pattern shako in general use by the infantry. Authorised by General Order 65 of June 1869, the headdress was replaced by the home service helmet in 1878. The plate, a universal crowned wreath and Garter, has the regimental badge and number displayed in the centre.

24 The regiment's Lamb device is featured here at the top of a strap inscribed with the words 'Queen's Royal'. Within this is the regimental number. Worn by other ranks in the glengarry cap for the period 1874 to 1881, the badge is in die-stamped brass. *(Photo courtesy of Coldstream Military Antiques)*

3rd (East Kent) Regiment

25 Sketch of an officers' oval silver shoulder-belt plate from *(Military) Shoulder-Belt Plates and Buttons* by Major HG Parkyn. Taken from an item on display at the Regimental Museum, the illustration shows the regiment's Dragon badge perched upon a strap inscribed with the regimental motto, Veteri frondescit honore (Its ancient honour flourishes).

26 Following the embarkation of the three regiments of Foot Guards for France in February 1793, the 3rd Regiment were directed to proceed to Windsor in order to undertake public duties. In this original watercolour painting by Edward Dayes, the artist shows a private of the regiment against a backdrop of the Round Tower of Windsor Castle. He is shown wearing an all-brass oval shoulder-belt plate with the design of the number '3' surmounted by a crown. *(Image courtesy of the Anne SK Brown Military Collection, Brown University Library)*

27 This rectangular gilt officers' plate shows a silver crowned strap inscribed with the motto Veteri frondescit honore (Its ancient honour flourishes). This was not mentioned in the Royal Warrant regarding clothing and badges in 1751, but nevertheless had appeared on the Colours around that date. Within the strap, the regimental number is surmounted by its ancient dragon badge. There are two battle honours, 'Peninsula' and 'Douro, the former having been authorised on 6 April 1815, the latter less than two years prior to that on 10 September 1813. This particular specimen appeared on the sales list of The Military Campaign which offered it complete with its original leather liner. Approximately the same shape as the plate, the liner carries the ink inscription, 'WFW 3rd Buffs', the initials possibly those of an officer owner. A short-lived item dated at around 1830. *(Photo courtesy of The Military Campaign)*

28 The headdress shown in this original watercolour painting of an officer by Reginald Augustus Wymer (1849-1935) dates the period of the picture around the time of the Regency shako of 1816 to 1829. In 1822 there had been a change in the style of plate used by the officers. 'The badge', according to Kipling and King, 'now consisting of an ornamented star usually silver but occasionally gilt and which, in addition to the regiment's number and special insignia, now carried the many battle-honours which had been awarded the previous year.' The subject of the painting has been given a bright gilt oblong shoulder-belt plate which clearly includes a silver Dragon device. Unusually, however, the beast appears facing upwards, instead of from left to right. *(Image courtesy of the Anne SK Brown Military Collection, Brown University Library)*

4th (The King's Own) Regiment

29 Sketch of the other ranks' shoulder-belt plate introduced around 1784. In brass, the word 'King's' appears at the top, and 'Own' at the bottom. In the middle, a crown over the regimental Lion badge.

30 Sketch of an officers' oval gilt shoulder-belt plate introduced, according to Volume 1 of Colonel LI Cowper's history of the regiment (Oxford University Press, 1939), in 1792.

31 This officers' silver and gilt shoulder-belt plate is mentioned by Colonel LI Cowper in his 1939 two-volume history of the King's Own with a date of 1833. The regiment's ancient Lion badge, said to have been granted in the time of William III, is featured above 'IV' within a crowned strap inscribed 'The King's Own Regiment'. On either side is a silver wreath of laurels which terminates to meet a collection of nine battle honour scrolls at the bottom: 'Corunna', 'St Sebastian', 'Badajoz', 'Nive', 'Salamanca', 'Waterloo', 'Peninsula', 'Vittoria' and 'Bladensburg'. The regiment had been known as 'The Queen's' for many years and was re-designated as 'King's Own' after the death of Queen Anne in 1714. *(Photo courtesy of Noble Numismatics)*

32 A fine plate of gilt and silver worn by officers of the regiment on the shako introduced in 1829 and in use until 1844. The Lion of England sits within the Garter which is placed upon an eight-pointed silver star. *(Photo courtesy of Les Martin)*

33 Major HG Parkyn places this other ranks' die-struck shoulder-belt plate as having being worn between 1812 and 1820. The Lion and regimental number are featured in the centre of a strap displaying the title 'The King's Own Regiment'. *(Photo courtesy of Noble Numismatics)*

34 From the John Player 1931 'Military Headdress' series of cigarette cards, a fair representation of an officers' forage cap with Lion and regimental number badge.

35 One of a collection of hand-coloured aquatint plates after Edward Dayes featuring an officer of the 4th Regiment wearing the oval shoulder-belt plate illustrated at 30. *(Image courtesy of the Anne SK Brown Military Collection, Brown University Library)*

4TH REGIMENT OF FOOT;
Officer's forage cap, 1852-1881.

5th (Northumberland) (Fusiliers) Regiment

36 Here we have a sketch of an early silver oval officers' shoulder-belt plate featuring a St George and the Dragon together with the Latin motto *Quo fata vocant* (Wherever fate calls).

37 In this hand-coloured plate dated 1835 from the Richard Cannon history of the regiment, St George killing the Dragon and roses appear quite clear on both Colours. Fusilier grenade badges, on the caps, shoulder-belt plates and as a pack badge, are also much in evidence.

38 A hand-coloured plate dated 1837 showing an officer wearing the oblong, gilt and silver, shoulder-belt plate worn prior to 1855. A more detailed sketch of this item appears on page 87 of Major HG Parkyn's book, *(Military) Shoulder-Belt Plates and Buttons* and shows that the ball of the grenade had St George and the Dragon in the centre of a strap inscribed with the motto Quo fata vocant (Wherever fate calls), surrounded by a wreath interlaced with scrolls bearing battle honours.

39 In this original watercolour painting by Richard Simkin, signed and dated 1881, we have a detailed example of a drummer wearing the 'Waterloo' shako of 1812 to 1816. Unclear in the image is any detail of the brass plate worn, but records reveal that this would have had the Royal Cypher above the regimental number '5'. The shoulder-belt plate, also lacking detail, is oval and appears to have a grenade device. *(Image courtesy of the Anne SK Brown Military Collection, Brown University Library)*

40 From the Anne SK Brown Military Collection, an original watercolour featuring four officers wearing undress uniforms. Dated from 1836 to 1880, the figures all wear caps with grenade badges above the number '5'. *(Image courtesy of the Anne SK Brown Military Collection, Brown University Library)*

41 The other ranks' brass glengarry badge for the period 1874 to 1881. The number '5' has been pierced in the centre of a strap inscribed with the regimental motto. *(Photo courtesy of Coldstream Military Antiques)*

42 This hand-coloured aquatint drawn by Edward Dayes and published on 1 December 1792 shows the officer on the left wearing a silver gorget engraved with the Royal Arms. A white shoulder-belt supports the sword, and this is shown with an oval silver plate similar to illustration 36. The figure of St George and the Dragon, however, faces in the opposite direction. A plain Roman 'V' for all the buttons, the soldier on the right having instead '5'.

THE NORTHUMBERLAND FUSILIERS, OFFICERS, UNDRESS UNIFORM, 1836 – 1880

Fifth or the Northumberland Regiment of Foot 1673

6th (Royal 1st Warwickshire) Regiment

43 A sketch from Edward Almack's book, Regimental Badges Worn in the British Army One Hundred Years Ago (Blades, East & Blades, London, 1900). The book deals with a collection of drawings found by Almack in an old silversmith's notebook. The silversmith's notes accompanying the image (I have amended the spelling and punctuation) are as follows: 'The 6 or first Warwickshire Regt. silver polished plate, metal gilt triangular border, metal gilt garter & crown with buckle, the garter pierced motto (VI or 1st Warwickshire Regt), within the garter on a blue enamelled silver plate, a silver cast antelope, the chain and ground of which is gilt and burnished, the antelope dead silver. The edges of the garter knurled.' As we can see, what the silversmith refers to as a 'garter', is in fact a strap.

44 In this original watercolour painting by Captain Edwin Hewgill, the officer is most likely wearing the shoulder-belt plate illustrated at 43. The artist's inclusion of '1673' in his caption refers to the formation of the regiment, and not that of the period depicted in the image. *(Image courtesy of the Anne SK Brown Military Collection, Brown University Library)*

45 The 6th Regiment had received the geographical title of '1st Warwickshire' in 1782 and here we see it on the oval brass shoulder-belt plate illustrated. The Antelope has been engraved above the Roman numerals 'VI' in the centre. It would not be until 1832, and while stationed at Poona in India, that the regiment received its 'Royal' title.

46 The illustration shows an example of the other ranks' one-piece plate worn on the shako authorised by General Order 65 of June 1869. A universal crowned laurel wreath in brass, the numeral '6' has been pierced within the centre of a Garter.

Sixth or the 1st Warwickshire Regiment of Foot 1673.
1792 by Capt. Hewgill.

47 Almost all of the sergeants posing in this photograph taken in India in 1871 wear a metal numeral '6' in their caps. A few, however, have the Antelope above. The number '6' also appears on the shoulder straps. *(Photo courtesy of Alan Seymour)*

7th (or Royal Fusiliers) Regiment

48 Colour plate after Captain H Oakes Jones featuring, from left to right: a miner, grenadier, colonel, fusilier and lieutenant for the period 1685 to 1690. The artist has included two examples of cannon bearing the device of a rose within a crowned Garter, later to be the regimental badge.

49 Illustrated is a detail from one of the fine colour plates included with Historical Records of the 7th or Royal Regiment of Fusiliers by Lieutenant-Colonel Percy Groves. Illustrated by the author, the book was published in 1903 by Frederick B Guerin. Here we a have a faithful reproduction of a fine Rocco-style shoulder-belt-plate for which Colonel Groves notes: '… the battle-honours were inscribed on the laurel-leaves on the slide [the horizontal bar just below the plate]. This handsome Belt-plate, &c., was introduced, we believe, about 1830-2, and was worn by Officers and Staff-Sergeants of the Royal Fusiliers until the introduction of the tunic [in 1855].' Just below the plate, the battle honours on the slide were 'Minden', 'Egmont Op Zee' and 'Martinique'. Almost entirely covered by the regiment's crowned United Red and White Rose badge, the blue enamel band running from top left to bottom right is, in fact, a Garter belt.

The Sergeants 1st Royal Regiment - Peshawar 1871

50 A detailed original painting by Thomas Charles Wageman of an unnamed officer who wears the shoulder-belt plate shown in illustration 49. *(Image courtesy of the Anne SK Brown Military Collection, Brown University Library)*

51 In this colour plate of uniform after Percy Groves, we see included a representation of the silver and gilt ornament worn on the officers' epaulette straps. The fur cap plates bear the Royal Arms. The officers' plate is that illustrated and described on page 15 of Almack's book: '…square, burnished dead gilt and with a cast metal gilt Garter crown & Rose in centre.' For the fusilier on the right, an oval engraved plate of which Major Parkyn describes as being in brass and 'worn by other ranks during the Peninsular and Waterloo period.'

52 The artist of this original watercolour, Richard Caton Woodville, shows an officer of the regiment about 1828 wearing a large gilt grenade in his fur cap. There is no detail apparent, but on the ball of the grenade would have been a crowned Garter with a rose in the centre. Just below the buckle of the Garter, the number '7'. An oblong, gilt shoulder-belt plate is also worn, this having the same device as the cap. *(Image courtesy of the Anne SK Brown Military Collection, Brown University Library)*

53 An officers' forage cap badge. The flames of the grenade seem to have been detached, the numeral '7' in gold wire separate below. *(Photo courtesy of Cultman Collectables)*

8th (The King's) Regiment

54 Sketch from *(Military) Shoulder-belt Plates and Buttons* by Major HG Parkyn showing the officers' plate worn prior to 1855. In burnished gilt, the White Horse is in silver on a crimson velvet ground. The word 'King's' appears in Old English lettering directly below the crown.

55 Richard Simkin's painting of an officer in 1832 has the shako of the period 1829 to 1844. Kipling and King describe two plates for this time (1) 'On the universal plate; A silver star on which a wreath and within it a circlet inscribed Nec aspera terrent (By difficulties undaunted). In the centre, the White Horse of Hanover above the Roman numerals VIII. Above the circlet a scroll inscribed King's and above this the Sphinx superscribed Egypt.' (2) 'An eight-pointed star, the topmost point displaced by a Victorian crown. On the star, the Garter surmounted by a tablet inscribed King's. In the centre the White Horse on ground and below this the Roman numerals VIII.'

Also worn is a gilt shoulder-belt plate with silver mounts. Most likely this is the plate that had the White Horse in the centre of a crowned Garter and a scroll inscribed with the battle honour 'Niagara'. *(Image courtesy of the Anne SK Brown Military Collection, Brown University Library)*

56 An officers' gilt and silver shako plate for the period 1869-1878 is illustrated. A universal crowned laurel wreath and Garter in gilt, the White Horse appears on a bar above the Roman numerals 'VIII' on a scarlet cloth backing.

8th The King's Regiment
1832.

9th (The East Norfolk) Regiment

57 In this double engraved plate after Edward Dayes (1763-1804), the officer on the left is shown wearing an oval silver plate with a high beaded rim. In the centre is the figure of Britannia. For the soldier on the right, the plate was in brass and with a crown above Britannia.

58 Regarding the plate illustrated, Major HG Parkyn comments: 'About 1820 the officers' plates were oblong, silver, with rounded corners, and the design in relief of Britannia on a label inscribed 'IX Regt', The other ranks' plates were of the same design, but stamped brass.' Illustrated here is an other ranks' version from the saleroom of Noble Numismatics. *(Photo courtesy of Noble Numismatics)*

59 An original unsigned watercolour painting of an officer of the 9th Regiment dated 1835. He wears the large crowned star shako plate of the period, and an oblong gilt shoulder-belt plate bearing the figure of Britannia. *(Image courtesy of the Anne SK Brown Military Collection, Brown University Library)*

60 An officer of the 9th Regiment, his forage cap having the figure of Britannia above the numeral '9'.

10th (North Lincoln) Regiment

61 Edward Almack's book, Regimental Badges Worn in the British Army One Hundred Years Ago, was first published in 1900 and shows on page 17 a sketch of an unusual design of shoulder-belt plate belonging to the 10th Regiment. Of a crescent shape, the item has the number '10' within a beaded circle. The notes accompanying the plate record how it was 'A silver polished plate doomed high where the number is pined on.'

62 Sketch from *(Military) Shoulder-Belt Plates and Buttons* by Major HG Parkyn who dates this item as 1830 to 1836. In gilt, the oblong shoulder-belt plate shows the regimental number within a strap inscribed 'North Lincoln'. Below this is the Sphinx over 'Egypt'. A crowned wreath of laurels surrounds the strap. Below the crown is the battle honour for the Peninsular War, and below the Sphinx, that for the Battle of Sobraon which took place on 10 February 1846.

63 An unsigned watercolour painting featuring an officer of the 10th Regiment. He wears the Waterloo shako with tall green plume and gilt plate, and an oval gilt sword-belt plate. *(Image courtesy of the Anne SK Brown Military Collection, Brown University Library)*

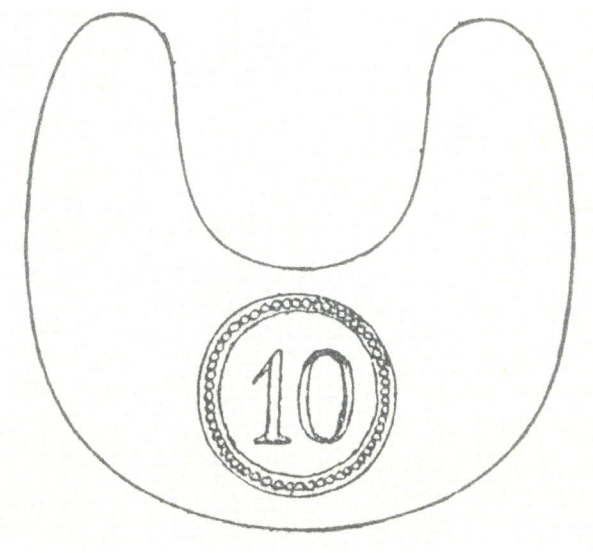

11th (North Devon) Regiment

64 The plate illustrated was worn on the 'Waterloo' shako of 1812 to 1816. Of a universal pattern, without a special regimental badge the item displays a reversed and intertwined 'GR' cypher above the Roman numerals 'XI'. *(Photo courtesy of Noble Numismatics)*

65 An officers' waist-belt clasp worn between 1855 and 1881 is illustrated. The centre has a crown and number in silver on a gilt background, the circle also in silver and with the 'North Devon Regiment' title assumed in 1782. *(Photo courtesy of Noble Numismatics)*

66 Sketch of an oblong shoulder-belt plate with rounded corners. The 'North Devon' title appears within the centre of an eight-pointed star, and four Peninsular War battle honours—'Nivelle', Peninsula', 'Toulouse' and 'Salamanca'—authorised during 1815 and 1816—are shown on an oval.

12th (East Suffolk) Regiment

67 Colonel Webb notes that the shoulder-belt plate illustrated was in use between 1799 and 1815 and was the earliest that could be traced to the regiment. A gilt oval, the strap, crown and 'Gibraltar' are in silver, the numeral in gilt. Lieutenant-Colonel EAH Webb, author of History of the 12th (The Suffolk) Regiment 1685-1913.

68 The officers' shako plate for the period 1815 to 1828—a silver star. On this is a laurel wreath surrounding a crowned gilt oval inscribed with the battle honours 'Minden', Gibraltar and 'Seringapatam'.

69 A similar design to the shako plate shown at illustration 68, this time in the centre of the officers' gilt shoulder-belt plate of 1825 to 1842.

70 In this colour plate after PW Reynolds the shako plate illustrated at 68 and shoulder-belt plate at 69 can be seen being worn.

71 From Colonel Webb's history, the officers' shoulder-belt plate introduced in 1843 and worn until March 1855 when breastplates were abolished. Of bright burnished gilt with silver mountings.

72 A photographic plate from Colonel Webb's history illustrating two officers' shako plates: that worn between 1800 and 1806 (left), the other in use from 1806 to 1815 (right).

73 Shako plate worn by officers of battalion companies on the Bell-topped shako of 1829 to 1843.

74 Another shako plate for the period 1829 to 1843; this time that worn by officers of the regiment's light companies. Colonel Webb notes that the 12th was '…one of those that were specially select in having a light company shako star for this head-dress of a particular pattern…'

75 Here from Colonel Webb's history we have three plates for the shako authorised by Horse Guards Circular Memorandum of 4 December 1843. In this so-called 'Albert Shako', from left to right, the plates are officers' patterns for the grenadier company, battalion companies and light company.

76 In this photographic plate from Colonel Webb's book we have examples of the officers' shako plates for 1855 to 1861 and 1861 to 1870 (top), and a forage cap badge (centre). At the bottom is the officers' shako plate which was introduced in 1871 and worn until the introduction of the home service helmet (bottom right) in 1878.

77 The officers' shako plate shown at the bottom of illustration 76. *(Photo courtesy of Coldstream Military Antiques)*

78 Here we have an example of the glengarry badge introduced in 1874 for other ranks which Lieutenant-Colonel EAH Webb describes as 'a twelve-pointed star, surmounted by a unique castle, with three turrets and key.' The key, in fact, had been placed perilously on the top of the central turret of the castle instead of the more usual position in front of the doorway. But, as Colonel Webb points out, this made the key 'so frail it was easily broken…' Indeed, the otherwise perfect specimen illustrated seems to have suffered that fate, as only the bottom section of the key remains intact.

79 An early photograph showing the regimental band of the 12th Regiment in which the metal number '12' is being worn in the caps of most of the musicians. Also note the same number on the shoulder straps. *(Photo courtesy of Alan Seymour)*

80 Four examples of officers' waist-belt clasps from Colonel Webb's regimental history.

OFFICERS' WAISTBELT CLASPS.
NO. 2 WORN BY FIELD RANKS ONLY.
(*Exact sizes.*)

13th (1st Somersetshire) (Prince Albert's Regiment of Light Infantry)

81 From Coldstream Military Antiques, a fine example of an officers' waist-belt clasp manufactured by Jennens & Co. The title 'Prince Alberts Light Infantry' appears in silver on the circle, the seeded gilt centre having a strung bugle surmounted by a mural crown and with 'XIII' within the strings. *(Photo courtesy of Coldstream Military Antiques)*

82 An officers' forage cap badge of gold and silver embroidery on black Melton cloth. *(Photo courtesy of Coldstream Military Antiques)*

83 Photograph of Major Richard Cooper wearing the forage cap badge illustrated at 82. Major Cooper's first commission with the regiment was dated 8 July 1869.

84 The other ranks' all brass shako plate of 1869 to 1878. *(Photo courtesy of Cultman Collectables)*

85 The Colours, presented from the hand of His Royal Highness Prince Albert at Southsea Common on Thursday 13 August 1846. Appearing on the Regimental Colour are both the Sphinx with 'Egypt' and Mural Crown with 'Jellalabad'.

Queen's Colour

Regimental Colour

14th (Buckinghamshire or The Prince of Wales's Own) Regiment

86 A fine shoulder-belt-plate, c1840 to 1855, from Bosley's Military Auctions which shows four of the regiment's battle honours on scrolls placed upon the leaves of a laurel wreath: 'Bhurtpore', 'Java', 'Tournay' and 'Corunna'. Just below the wreath, 'Waterloo' appears on a curved scroll, and seen in the centre of the plate with the word 'India' is the Royal Tiger. *(Photo courtesy of Bosley's Military Auctions)*

87 Major HG Parkyn in his important book, (Military) Shoulder-Belt-Plates and Buttons, records that 'An entirely new design was adopted the following year [1832] to show the Honours, including that of 'Bhurtpore'. He refers to the plate illustrated, a rectangular back plate with silver crown and number. The honours mentioned appear on scrolls placed upon a silver wreath: 'Coruna', 'Java', 'Waterloo' and of course, 'Bhurtpore''. This plate was worn until 1840. *(Photo courtesy of Bosley's Military Auctions)*

88 A fine watercolour portrait by James Gillray of Colonel Welbore Ellis Doyle of the 14th Regiment. The colonel is wearing a gorget and shoulder-belt plate, both bearing the number '14'. Major Parkyn describes the latter as 'The early officers' shoulder-belt plate was an oval silver polished one with the number 14 within a raised oval; the plate having a raised rim.' . Born in Ireland in 1758, Doyle had joined the 55th Regiment as an ensign in December 1770. He went on to serve with an American-raised formation styled as the 'Volunteers of Ireland', afterwards exchanging to a commission in the 14th Regiment in 1789. He became a major-general in 1795 and went on to command the troops in Ceylon, where he died in 1798. *(Image courtesy of the Anne SK Brown Military Collection, Brown University Library)*

89 The other ranks' glengarry badge worn from 1876 to 1881. On 26 May 1876 the 16th Regiment had been authorised to add 'The Prince of Wales's Own' to its title and here we see the Prince's Plumes, Coronet and motto in white metal at the top of the badge. The White Horse of Hanover, the ancient badge of the regiment, can be seen below. At the bottom, and appearing to hang from the buckle of the strap, is the Royal Tiger above 'India'.

90 A die-stamped brass bandsman's music case badge. *(Photo courtesy of Bosley's Military Auctions)*

91 Colour plate after PW Reynolds featuring a private of 1792. He wears an oval brass shoulder-belt with the number '14' in the centre.

92 Colour plate after PW Reynolds of an officer c1840 wearing the shoulder-belt plate shown at illustration 86. The shako authorised by Horse Guards Memorandum on 22 December 1828 and in use until 1844 is being worn. The plate comprised the universal crowned gilt star in the centre of which was a silver star upon which was a gilt strap inscribed 'Corunna', 'Waterloo' and 'Java'. This was surrounded by a laurel wreath. In the centre, the White Horse of Hanover with the Roman numerals 'XIV' below.

15th (York East Riding) Regiment

93 A sketch from *(Military) Shoulder-Belt Plates and Buttons* by Major HG Parkyn showing an officers' oval plate featuring a silver star on a gilt plate. In the centre, a red cross within a strap inscribed, '15 or Yorkshire E R Reg'.

94 A coloured lithographic plate after André Léon Larue Mansion featuring an officer c1831 who wears an oblong gilt and silver shoulder-belt plate displaying 'XV' within a crowned Garter. This is the plate illustrated on page 118 (item No 159) of Major HG Parkyn's *(Military) Shoulder-Belt Plates and Buttons*). The officer is wearing the Bell-topped shako of 1829 to 1844, the badge being: on the universal plate a diamond-cut silver star. On this a Maltese cross with on the top edge the battle honour 'Martinique', and on the bottom edge 'Guadaloupe'. Gilt lions between each arm of the cross, in the centre of which are the Roman numerals 'XV'. The print was published by William Spooner of 259 Regent Street, London. *(Image courtesy of the Anne SK Brown Collection, Brown University Library)*

95 The other ranks' die-struck brass glengarry badge for the period 1874 to 1881. *(Photo courtesy of Bosley's Military Auctions)*

16th (Bedfordshire) Regiment

96 Highly polished, this fine officers' rectangular plate has a representation of the Star of the Order of the Bath in cut silver, upon which has been set a crowned spray of laurel superimposed on a Maltese cross, all in gilt. In the centre, and on a ground of blue enamel, the regimental number appears foliated and surrounded by the word 'Bedfordshire' on a pierced circle. The 'Bedfordshire' part of this regiment's title was not assumed until 1809, some twenty-seven years after geographical designations had been conferred upon line infantry regiments as an aid to recruiting. It had originally been 'Buckinghamshire', but when Sir Henry Calvert became colonel of the 14th (Bedfordshire) Regiment in February 1802 he had requested that an exchange of titles be made with the 16th. The colonel had large estates in Buckinghamshire and his wish was eventually granted in 1809. *(Photo courtesy of The Military Campaign)*

97 A fine officers' example of the gilt and silver plate worn on the shako authorised by a General Order dated 10 August 1815. *(Photo courtesy of The Military Campaign)*

98 An officers' plate for the Regency shako of 1816 to 1829. The regimental number appears on a ground of white enamel enclosed within a crowned gilt circle. The crown is inlayed with crimson velvet. The eight-pointed facetted star is silver. *(Photo courtesy of The Military Campaign)*

99 From the Anne SK Brown Military Collection, a fine unsigned miniature painting on ivory of an unnamed officer of the 16th Regiment dated c1832. The shoulder-belt ornament, with its oblong plate and silver mountings, appears authentic, but is not illustrated or described in Parkyn. For the headdress, a fair representation of the Bell-topped shako authorised by Horse Guards Circular Memorandum dated 22 December 1828, but once again, the plate is not recognisable. *(Image courtesy of the Anne SK Brown Military Collection, Brown University Library)*

100 The plate for the Bell-topped shako is recorded by Kipling and King as follows: 'On the universal plate: A silver star and on this in gilt a Maltese cross surmounted by a crown. On the cross a laurel-wreath within which is a circlet inscribed Bedfordshire. In the centre the numeral 16.' A fine specimen is illustrated. *(Photo courtesy of Bosley's Military Auctions)*

101 The universal plate for the infantry shako introduced by General Order 65 of June 1869 and worn until the introduction of the home service helmet in 1878. *(Photo courtesy of Bosley's Military Antiques)*

17th (Leicestershire) Regiment

102 Here we have the officers' shoulder-belt plate taken into use in 1831 and consisting of a silver diamond-cut star on a plate of dead gilt, silver crown and silver numeral 'XVII'. In the centre, the Royal Tiger with 'Hindoostan' below (unusually) the Tiger, both in dead gilt. *(Photo courtesy of Noble Numismatics)*

103 Lieutenant-Colonel EAH Webb's, A History of the Services of the 17th (The Leicestershire) Regiment records this officers' shako plate as being in use between 1829 and 1845. The Royal Tiger with 'Hindoostan' above and regimental number below is in dead gilt and has been placed upon an eight-pointed silver, diamond-cut star. The crowned back plate is in dead gilt. *(Photo courtesy of Noble Numismatics)*

104 In silver and gilt, the officers' waist-belt plate worn from 1855 to 1881. *(Photo courtesy of The Military Campaign)*

105 Plate from Lieutenant-Colonel EAH Webb's regimental history showing three shoulder-belt plates worn by officers. On the left, with '17' within a crowned circle, is the oval plate of the 1st Battalion in use between 1799 to 12 October 1825. The sketch of the plate for 1776 has the Royal Cypher 'GR' and a beaded edge. For the 2nd Battalion (raised in 1799 and disbanded in 1802), the plate on the right has a wreath surrounding a crown over the regimental number. Colonel Webb gives a date of 1799 to 1802 for this item.

106 Plate from Lieutenant-Colonel EAH Webb's regimental history showing two officers' shako plates. On the left that in use between 1815 to 12 October 1825, and on the right the replacement pattern which was worn until 1828.

107 From Colonel Webb's regimental history of the 17th, two officers' shako plates. On the left, that for 1855, and on the right the smaller version of 1861.

108 Two officer' items, the shako plate of 1871 to 1879 (top), and at the bottom, the helmet plate introduced in 1879 and worn until 30 June 1881. Photographic plate from Colonel Webb's history.

109 The Colours of 1848, and the Royal Tiger badge.

110 Two officers' items: the shako plate for 1846 to 1855 (left), and the shoulder-belt plate (right) worn for the same period.

111 The officers' shako plate for 1843 to 1845 (left), and a shoulder-belt plate of 1843 to 1845 (right).

112 From Colonel Webb's regimental history, three officers' waistbelt clasps. At the top, the rectangular pattern worn c1831, in the centre the type introduced in 1855, and at the bottom that for 1845. Both the top and bottom items were worn by field ranks only.

18th (Royal Irish) Regiment

113 The other ranks' shoulder-belt plate worn prior to 1855. The Crown and Harp are seen in the centre of a wreath of thistles, roses and shamrocks, the motto appearing on a three-part scroll above. Below the wreath is the Sphinx over 'Egypt' and below that a scroll inscribed 'XVIII Royal Irish'. *(Photo courtesy of Noble Numismatics)*

114 A fine example of the other ranks' plate worn on the shako authorised by General Order 65 of June 1869 and worn until the introduction of the home service helmet in 1878. *(Photo courtesy of Bosley's Military Auctions)*

19th (1st York North Riding) Princess of Wales's Own Regiment

115 Sketch from *(Military) Shoulder-Belt Plates and Buttons* by Major HG Parkyn which refers to this gilt plate, with its 'XIX' within an oval and grenade device, as having been '…ascribed to 1816-1825', and worn by the regiment's grenadier company.

116 Colour plate after PW Reynolds showing a drummer and bandsman of 1852. Both wear the shako authorised by Horse Guards Circular Memorandum of 4 December 1843, the universal plates having the regimental number within a crowed circular wreath of half oak, half laurel.

20th (East Devonshire) Regiment

117 This fine example of an officers' shoulder-belt plate has been dated at c1830 to 1855. All in gilt with a frosted back plate, the simple fittings show a crowned wreath with the regimental number in Roman numerals in the centre. The particular plate illustrated is from the superb stock held by The Military Campaign and was advertised as being attributed to a Major James Birch Sharpe. Major Sharpe was severely wounded at Inkerman and died from his wounds at Scutari Hospital on 29 December 1854. *(Photo courtesy of The Military Campaign)*

21st (Royal Scots Fusiliers) Regiment

118 A sketch from Almack's book of 1900 which dealt with badges worn one hundred years before that. Taken from a silversmith's records of the time, the description accompanying the sketch notes that the item was of cast metal with the motto in raised letters on a mottled ground. The crown, thistle and number were of a dead gilt and the centre of the plate was burnished.

119 A sketch of the officers' gilt with silver grenade shoulder-belt plate of 1830 to 1846.

120 A detailed colour print after George Kruger of a 21st Regiment sergeant. Grenade badges can be seen on the collar and fur cap, the oblong shoulder-belt plate being similar to the officers' of 1830 to 1846 — a grenade, on the ball of which has the number '21' within a crowned circle engraved with the motto *Nec aspera terrent* (By difficulties undaunted).

121 The glengarry, along with special badges, was introduced as an undress cap in 1874. With its 'Royal North British Fusiliers' title, we can assume that this particular badge was worn from 1874 until 1877 when the title of the regiment was amended to '21st (Royal Scots Fusiliers) Regiment of Foot'. Kipling and King, in their most valuable book, confirm the existence of badges identical to the one illustrated here, but with the new title engraved on the strap.
(Photo courtesy of Coldstream Military Antiques)

22nd (Cheshire) Regiment)

122 Dated at around 1820, this superb example of an officers' shoulder-belt plate takes the form of a polished gilt oblong plate upon which has been placed a silver star with square ends to the rays. And on this, a crowned circle in gilt within which appears a wreath enclosing the regimental number. All is in gilt and on a ground of blue enamel. Three battle honours appear below the star: 'Scinde', 'Meeanee' and 'Hyderabad'. *(Photo courtesy of The Military Campaign)*

123 From the Anne SK Brown Military Collection, an original unsigned ink and watercolour painting of an 'officer c1790' in which the artist includes a plain oblong gilt shoulder-belt plate with the number '22'. *(Image courtesy of the Anne SK Brown Military Collection, Brown University Library)*

124 From Almack's book, a sketch of an early oval shoulder-belt plate described as matted gilt with silver star and raised rim.

23rd (Royal Welsh Fusiliers) Regiment

125 Colour plate from the Clothing Book of 1742 clearly showing the Prince of Wales's insignia being worn on the front of a grenadier's cap.

126 A sketch of an officers' gilt plate, with the feathers in silver, from *(Military) Shoulder-Belt Plates and Buttons* and dated as circa 1800.

127 An original watercolour painting by W Sharpe featuring an officer wearing the Albert shako authorised by Horse Guards Circular Memorandum of 4 December 1843. A large gilt fused grenade with the Prince of Wales's insignia on the ball covers almost the entire front of the headdress. *(Image courtesy of the Anne SK Brown Military Collection, Brown University Library)*

24th (2nd Warwickshire) Regiment

128 Here we have an exhibit from the Museum of the South Wales Borderers in the form of a fine example of the officers' shako authorised by General Order 65 of June 1869 and worn by infantry regiments until the introduction of the home service helmet in 1878. The universal crowned wreath plate is in gilt and displays the number '24' within the Garter. Below the Garter and on the bottom joint of the wreath is the Sphinx over a tablet inscribed 'Egypt'.

129 An officers' waist-belt, the clasp showing the '2nd Warwickshire' title adopted in 1782 and in use until 1881. Another item from the collection of the South Wales Borderers Museum at Brecon.

130 Sheet music cover for 'The Noble 24th', a song written by CC Anewick (music by Vincent Davies) commemorating the services of the regiment during the Zulu War of 1879. The artist has been careful to include the regimental number '24' at the centre of the helmet plate and Colour. *(Image courtesy of the Anne SK Brown Military Collection, Brown University Library)*

131 Possibly one of the most attractive and sought after shoulder-belt plates of all is the officers' item illustrated. Rococo in style, it has a band of blue enamel winding its way down from the top of the plate to the bottom righthand corner. Gilt letters have been placed upon it which in three sections spell out an interrupted version of the regimental motto, In veritate religionis confide (I trust in the truth of my conscience). The motto was given to the regiment in 1805 by King George III upon the occasion of its inclusion in its title of 'The King's Own Borderers'. The Royal Crest also came with the title change and this can be seen above two ovals, one charged with a representation of Edinburgh Castle and its motto Nisi dominus frustra (Unless the Lord be with us all is in vain), the other displaying the White Horse of Hanover and yet a third motto, Nec aspera terrent (By difficulties undaunted). Here too, and in silver, is the Sphinx over 'Egypt' awarded for service during the 1801 campaign in Egypt and authorised on 6 July of the following year.

25th (The King's Own Borderers) Regiment

132 The officer in this unsigned watercolour has been given a shako of the 1829 to 1844 period. The large, crowned star plate has a clear suggestion of '25' on a blue ground. *(Image courtesy of the Anne SK Brown Collection, Brown University Library)*

133 The officers' pre-1881 waist-belt clasp. *(Photo courtesy of Les Martin)*

134 The other ranks' plate for the shako authorised by General Order 65 of June 1869 and worn by infantry regiments until the introduction of the home service helmet in 1878. *(Photo courtesy of Coldstream Military Collectables)*

26th (Cameronians) Regiment

135 For this original watercolour painting by Richard Simkin, the artist gives a caption date of 1833. The Bell-topped shako of 1829 to 1844 is being worn, the large, crowned star plate having the regimental number in the centre. *(Image courtesy of the Anne SK Brown Collection, Brown University Library)*

136 Another watercolour from Richard Simkin, this time with a caption date of 1841. As in illustration 135 the Bell-topped shako is being worn, but this time Simkin has included the circular plate surmounted by a crown which replaced the star at the beginning of 1839. This change had been notified via a Horse Guards Circular Letter dated 22 February. The shoulder-belt plate worn at the time featured a Mullet star surrounded by a laurel wreath. The uppermost point of the star supported a crown and displayed the Sphinx over 'Egypt'. At the bottom, where the wreath joins, is a scroll inscribed 'Corunna', and below that 'China' above a Dragon. *(Image courtesy of the Anne SK Brown Collection, Brown University Library)*

137 An example of an officers' silver and gilt waist-belt clasp. *(Photo courtesy of Bosley's Military Auctions)*

27th (Inniskilling) Regiment

138 Sketch from page 574 of the history of the Royal Inniskilling Fusiliers compiled under the direction of a regimental historical records committee and published by Constable & Co Ltd in 1928. On the previous page the authors write that 'Between 1790 and 1810, or thereabouts, the majority of the officers' breast-plates, and of the men's as far as we know of them, were oval in form…' The plate was of dead gilt with beaded border, the castle, number and 'Inniskilling' being mounted in silver. The castle, a representation of the sixteenth-century structure at Inniskilling, County Fermanagh, is the regiment's ancient badge and was mentioned in the Royal Warrant of 1751.

139 In this unsigned watercolour painting of an officer of the 27th Regiment, the white shoulder-belt has an oblong gilt and silver plate similar to the type illustrated on page 156 of *(Military) Shoulder-Belt Plates and Buttons* — the Castle of Inniskilling above the number '27' within a crowned wreath. *(Image courtesy of the Anne SK Brown Military Collection, Brown University Library)*

140 A matted gilt shoulder-belt plate to the 27th Regiment which has a diamond-cut crowned silver star upon which has been placed the Castle of Inniskilling, the number '27' and the Sphinx, all in gilt. Ten of the star's rays are also in gilt, and these bear the following battle honours: 'Maida', 'Badajoz', 'Salamanca', 'Vittoria', 'Pyrenees', 'Nivelle', 'Orthes', 'Toulouse', 'Peninsula' and 'Waterloo'. *(Photo courtesy of Les Martin)*

141 A fine example of an officers' light company plate worn on the Regency shako of 1816 to 1829. On a silver star, a crowned gilt pierced strap with the word 'Enniskillen'. There is a gilt bugle in the centre upon a ground of dark green enamel. Below the strap, and in gilt, the Sphinx on a tablet inscribed 'Egypt'. *(Photo courtesy of Bosley's Military Auctions)*

142 This is the plate worn on the Albert shako of 1844 to 1855. Upon a crowned star of twelve points has been placed the number '27' within a strap inscribed 'Inniskilling'. Around this is a two-part wreath of laurel (left) and palm (right). Above the wreath are the Castle of Inniskilling and the Sphinx on a tablet inscribed 'Egypt'. At the lower joining of the wreath is an inverted scroll inscribed Nec aspera terrent (By difficulties undaunted) in Old English lettering and below that, the White Horse of Hanover. Inscribed upon the main rays of the star are the following battle honours: 'St Lucia', 'Toulouse', 'Vittoria', 'Waterloo', 'Nivelle', 'Salamanca', 'Maida', 'Pyrenees', 'Badajoz', 'Orthes' and 'Peninsula'. *(Photo courtesy of Les Martin)*

143 With the Inniskilling Castle on top of a strap, here we have the other ranks' glengarry badge of 1874 to 1881. *(Photo courtesy of Bosley's Military Antiques)*

28th (North Gloucestershire) Regiment

144 Thanks to a comprehensive article by Lieutenant-Colonel RM Grazebrook (*Journal of the Society for Army Historical Research*, No 99, Autumn 1946) dealing with the Gloucestershire Regiment's back badge, we can date this item as 1830 to 1881. Worn, as the name suggests, at the back of the headdress, this distinction commemorates the gallantry of the 28th during the Battle of Alexandria in 1801 when it was attacked both from the front and rear by French forces. *(Photo courtesy of Coldstream Military Antiques)*

145 The other ranks' glengarry badge, 1874 to 1881, which has the Sphinx above a tablet inscribed 'Egypt'. Authorised 6 July 1802, the honour was in recognition of the services of the 28th during the campaign of the previous year. *(Photo courtesy of Coldstream Military Antiques)*

146 The other ranks' plate for the Albert shako authorised by Horse Guards Circular of 4 December 1843 and worn until 1855. *(Photo courtesy of Bosley's Military Auctions)*

29th (Worcestershire) Regiment

147 A fine example of the shako plate worn by officers of the 29th between 1846 and 1855. All in gilt, the crowned eight-pointed star and laurel wreath feature the figure of lion standing on an heraldic wreath. Referring to the use of a lion, Major RW Bennett in his book Badges of the Worcestershire Regiment notes that the device was an ancient badge of the 29th and that 'Its earliest known appearance is on an officers' shoulder belt plate certainly before 1800.' *(Photo courtesy of Coldstream Military Antiques)*

148 Plate for the infantry shako authorised on 28 November 1860 and worn until 1869. *(Photo courtesy of Coldstream Military Antiques)*

149 From Bosley's Military Auctions, a superb example of the officers' shako authorised by General Order 65 of June 1869 and worn until the introduction of the home service helmet in 1878. *(Photo courtesy of Bosley's Military Antiques)*

150 A short-lived item, this officers' helmet plate would have been current from the introduction of the home service helmet in 1878 and the change of title to 'Worcestershire Regiment' in 1881. In the centre of a universal crowned star, wreath and Garter plate, the number '29' appears on a black leather backing. *(Photo courtesy of Coldstream Military Antiques)*

30th (Cambridgeshire) Regiment

151 Glengarry badge, 1874-1881, showing a Sphinx above a tablet inscribed 'Egypt' and the regimental number 'XXX' in Roman numerals. They appear in the centre of a strap inscribed with the Latin motto Spectemur Agendo (Let us be judged by our acts) which, although in use for a number of years, was not officially authorised until June 1911 (Army Order 150). The Sphinx had been awarded to the 30th Regiment for its services during the 1801 campaign in Egypt. *(Photo courtesy of Cultman Collectables)*

152 In this unsigned watercolour painting of an officer c1854, the forage cap has the regimental number in Roman numerals. *(Image courtesy of the Anne SK Brown Military Collection, Brown University Library)*

31st (Huntingdonshire) Regiment

153 Vast silverwork almost coverers the entire area of this magnificent officers' item. Tucked away among laurel leaves and scrolls charged with battle honours is a strap bearing the name 'Huntingdonshire'. Within this the precedence of the regiment in Roman numerals on a domed ground, and across the bottom of the strap the word 'Peninsula'. Huntingdonshire had been added to the regiment's title in 1782 as part of the scheme to aid recruiting. Topped by a crown, scrolls inscribed with the battle honours 'Orthes', 'Talavera', 'Albuhera', 'Vittoria', Pyrenees', Nivelle' and 'Nive' fall down both sides of the plate to where further honours, 'Cabool 1842', 'Moodkee', 'Ferozeshah', 'Aliwal' and 'Sobraon', appear in three lines. Major HG Parkyn puts a date on this item of '1847-1855'. *(Photo courtesy of The Military Campaign)*

154 An officers' plate worn on the shako introduced in 1861 and in use until 1869. A universal crowned star with the regimental number within the Garter. *(Photo courtesy of Coldstream Military Antiques)*

155 The other ranks' glengarry badge, 1874 to 1881. *(Photo courtesy of Coldstream Military Antiques)*

32nd (Cornwall) Regiment

156 Sketch from Military Insignia of Cornwall by D Endean Ivall and Charles Thomas. The authors note the item as being worn by officers in gilt or silver and '...seems to be shown in a portrait of an unknown officer...of the 32nd, in the period 1773-1783.'

33rd (The Duke of Wellington's) Regiment

157 The title engraved around the crowned strap of this officers' shoulder-belt-plate ('1st Yorkshire West Riding Regiment') was in use from 1782 until 1853. Long associated with the 33rd, both as its lieutenant-colonel and colonel, was the Duke of Wellington and upon his death in 1852 Her Majesty Queen Victoria was graciously pleased to confer upon the regiment the title of 33rd (Duke of Wellington's), along with the use of his crest and motto as a badge. With its fine central silver number and wreath, together with the double scroll that continues down from the strap buckle with the battle honours 'Seringapatam' and 'Waterloo', the currency of this item has been placed at between 1830 and 1855. *(Photo courtesy of The Military Campaign)*

158 An officers' gilt button displaying 'The Duke of Wellington's Regt.' on a circular strap. *(Photo courtesy of Coldstream Military Antiques)*

159 In gilt, an example of the plate worn on the shako introduced in 1861 and om use until 1869. *(Photo courtesy of Bosley's Military Auctions)*

160 An officers' waist-belt clasp with crowned 'VR' cypher and '33' in silver on a gilt late. *(Photo courtesy of Coldstream Military Antiques)*

34th (Cumberland) Regiment

161 This fine officers' shoulder-belt plate from the Coldstream Military Antiques sales list is in burnished gilt mounted with a facetted silver star upon which has been placed a gilt, crowned, Order of the Bath Cross. On the arms of the cross are seven battle honours: 'Peninsular' (top), 'Pyrenees' and 'Nive' (left), 'Vittoria' and 'Orthes' (right) and 'Nivelle' and 'Albuhera' (bottom). An eighth honour, 'Arroyo dos Molinos', is shown on a three-part scroll below the cross. The regimental number is in silver and appears at the centre within a circle inscribed 'Cumberland Regt.' *(Photo courtesy of Coldstream Military Antiques)*

162 The other ranks' glengarry badge of 1874 to 1881 is similar to the central device of the shoulder-belt plate illustrated at 161, but the battle honours 'Sevastopol' and 'Lucknow' have been added to the top arm of the cross. *(Photo courtesy of Bosley's Military Auctions)*

163 A fine officers' gilt shako plate for the period 1869 to 1878. *(Photo courtesy of Les Martin)*

35th (Dorsetshire) Regiment

164 The 35th Regiment held the subtitle 'Dorsetshire' from 1782 until 1805 when it changed to 'Sussex'. This sketch is taken from Almack's records which give a description of silver gilt with silver ornaments.

91

36th (Herefordshire) Regiment

165 This fine officers' shako plate from Coldstream Military Antiques was worn, according to Major Roger Bennett, circa 1825 to 1829. Mounted on a silver star is a gilt, crowned, continuous scroll inscribed 'Nivelle', 'Salamanca', 'Toulouse' and 'Peninsular'. A fifth battle honour, 'Vimiera', appears directly below the crown. In the centre, within two sprays of laurel, is the regimental number and the word 'Firm'. The origins of this motto, penned unusually in English, are obscure. Major Bennett recalls how the word had appeared on the regimental seal as early as 1773 and how permission to bear it on the Colours had to be obtained in 1817. *(Photo courtesy of Coldstream Military Antiques)*

166 From Almack's book, a sketch of the oval shoulder-belt plate worn c1800 described as: 'A metal gilt plate with silver beaded border. The beads burnished, a cast silver star polished. A metal gilt Garter lay'd up from the back of the star with a little edge to hold it down,' The title is 'on a matted ground, the letters burnished being raised above the ground. A silver crown and lion cast together, & number 36 boild dead, the centre of the plate matted.'

37th (North Staffordshire) Regiment

167 Sketch of the shoulder-belt plate worn up to 1855. In gilt, save for the regimental number which was in silver.

38th (1st Staffordshire) Regiment

168 Sketch from Almack's book of a polished silver plate c1800, the crown, number and Stafford knot being in gilt.

39th (Dorsetshire) Regiment

169 The central device on this magnificent example of an officers' shoulder-belt plate shows a silver-rayed star upon which has been placed a gilt crowned strap made up of red, blue and light green enamels. In the centre, and on a field of light green, the Castle, Key and Motto Montis insignia Calpe in gilt which commemorates the services of the 39th during the great siege of Gibraltar between 1779 and 1783. At the top of the plate and on a wide scroll, another motto, Primus in Indis, this recalling the regiment's justified claim that it was the first of the Line to serve in India. This distinction was re-authorised on 17 November 1835, having been discontinued about 1807. At the foot of the item, more honours: 'Plassey', 'Albuhera', 'Nive', 'Orthes', 'Nivelle', 'Pyrenees', 'Vittoria' and 'Peninsula'. *(Photo courtesy of The Military Campaign)*

170 Sketch from Almack's book who gives the following description: 'A metal gilt plate, with silver ornaments. A scroll half round quite plain. Number matted both boiled dead, underneath a label with motto (Gibraltar) on a matted ground raised letters boiled dead, the letters burnished.'

40th (2nd Somersetshire) Regiment

171 From Noble Numismatics, a superb example of the officers' shoulder-belt plate in use between 1844 and 1855. No less than fourteen battle honours appear on the squared-off rays of a silver star: 'Egypt', 'Monte Video', 'Roleia', 'Vimiera', 'Talavera', 'Badajoz', 'Salamanca', 'Waterloo', 'Vittoria', 'Pyrenees', 'Nivelle', 'Orthes', 'Toulouse' and 'Peninsula'. A gilt crowned wreath of laurels occupies the centre of the plate, around which have been placed a further four silver battle honour scrolls: 'Candahar', 'Cabool', 'Ghuznee 1842' and 'Maharajpore'. The regimental number in gilt is seen in the centre of a gilt strap inscribed '2nd Somersetshire'. *(Photo courtesy of Noble Numismatics)*

172 From the Anne SK Brown Military Collection, a full-length, unsigned, watercolour portrait of an officer. The artist provides good detail of both the shako and shoulder-belt plates. Of the former, this is the gilt crowned star type with '40' in the centre of a second star in silver, as worn on the Bell-topped shakos of 1829 to 1844. For the shoulder-belt plate, Major Parkyn illustrates this and shows it with '40' in the centre with a crowned scroll above inscribed '2nd Somersetshire'. All around are the rays of a star, thirteen of which have been engraved with battle honours. *(Image courtesy of the Anne SK Brown Military Collection, Brown University Library)*

41st (the Welsh) Regiment

173 In this portrait of Lieutenant-Colonel Robert Place by William Charles Ross, we have a clear representation of an officers' gilt shoulder-belt. An oval appears on an eight-pointed star which displays the Royal Arms, Garter and Roman numerals 'XLI'. Turning to page 153 of the regimental history written by Major AC Whitehorne and published in 1932, we read that 'Up to 1822 or 1823 the 41st was without a badge until the Union Badge, that of the Regiment of invalids, was restored to the Colours...Lieutenant-Colonel R Place, who had commanded for a short time in 1827, is shown in a portrait as wearing this badge on the breast-plate. This appears to be the only authentic instance of this badge being used on appointments from that day to this.' The regiment had, between 1751 and 1787, been known as the 41st Regiment of Invalids. *(Image courtesy of the Anne SK Brown Military Collection, Brown University Library)*

174 Published by William Spooner of 259 Regent Street, London, this colour lithograph features an officer of the 41st around 1831. The oblong gilt shoulder-belt plate worn displayed on a silver star the Prince of Wales's Plumes, Coronet and motto in silver on a blue enamel ground within the centre of a crowned Garter in gilt. The regimental number in Roman numerals, together with three battle honours: 'Queenstown', 'Niagara' and 'Ava' positioned below the Garter. The artists for the plate were Samuel Eschauzier and Henri Heidemans. *(Image courtesy of the Anne SK Brown Military Collection, Brown University Library)*

42nd Royal Highland (The Black Watch) Regiment

175 This coloured lithograph after Charles Frederick Brockdorff features an officer of the 42nd Regiment in Malta in 1840 wearing an oblong gilt and silver plate on his sword-belt. Major Parkyn illustrates the plate worn 1820 to 1845 which has '42' in the centre of a strap. Below this is the figure of St Andrew with his Cross, and below that the Sphinx on a tablet inscribed 'Egypt'. *(Image courtesy of the Anne SK Brown Military Collection, Brown University Library)*

176 Sketch from *(Military) Shoulder-Belt Plates and Buttons* of the other ranks' brass plate worn c1818 to 1830. The number is engraved within an oval in the centre of the Star of the Order of the Thistle.

97

43rd (Monmouthshire Light Infantry) Regiment

177 This officers' silver and gilt shoulder-belt plate, according to Major HG Parkyn, was in use between 1831 and 1855. The 43rd had taken on a light infantry role in 1803, the plate illustrated being one of several patterns to feature a crowned bugle with regimental number between the cords. *(Photo courtesy of Coldstream Military Antiques)*

178 An un-signed original watercolour featuring a portrait of an unnamed officer of the 43rd wearing the shoulder-belt plate illustrated at 177. *(Image courtesy of the Anne SK Brown Military Collection, Brown University Library)*

179 The other ranks' die-stamped brass glengarry badge c1874-1881. *(Photo courtesy of Coldstream Military Antiques)*

44th (East Essex) Regiment

180 For its services during the 1801 campaign, the 44th was awarded the Sphinx over 'Egypt' on 6 July of the following year. The oval shoulder-belt plate illustrated is from Major Parkyn's book who notes that it was silver with a raised rim and probably worn c1802. Note how the Sphinx has been placed at an unusual angle.

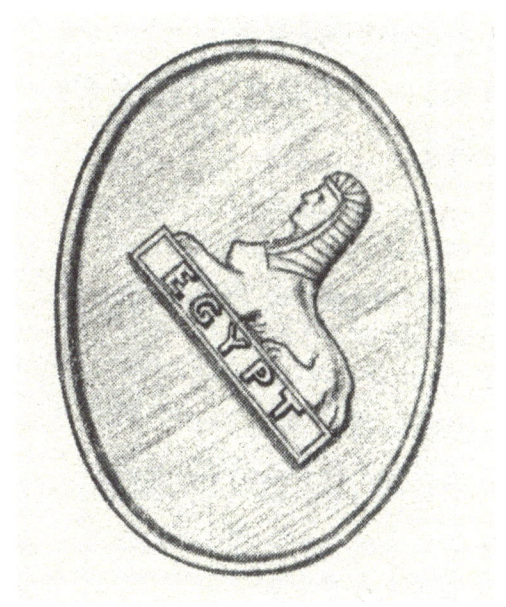

45th (Nottinghamshire Sherwood Foresters) Regiment

181 The officers' silver and gilt shoulder-belt plate adopted, according to Major Parkyn, in 1832. The regimental number appears in the centre of a crowned strap inscribed, '1st Nottinghamshire Regt'—'Sherwood Foresters' had not been added to the title until 1866. The battle honour 'Peninsular' on a scroll is shown below the strap, and thirteen others on the main rays of the star—'Roleia', 'Vimiera', 'Talavera', 'Busaco', 'Fuentes d' Onor', 'C Rodrigo', 'Badajoz', 'Salamanca', 'Vittoria', 'Pyrenees', 'Nivelle', 'Orthes' and 'Toulouse'. *(Photo courtesy of Les Martin)*

182 The other ranks' brass glengarry badge of 1874 to 1881. The regimental number and title have been included, 'Nottinghamshire' around the strap, 'Sherwood Foresters' on a double scroll at the bottom either side of a shield charged with the arms of Nottingham—a ragged cross and three crowns. *(Photo courtesy of Coldstream Military Antiques)*

183 Sketch from Almack's book of an oval shoulder-belt plate to the 45th. It is described as being all in silver.

46th (South Devonshire) Regiment

184 A detailed sketch from Military Insignia of Cornwall by D Endean Ivall and Charles Thomas showing an officers' shoulder-belt plate. The author's note that this pattern was probable the last to be worn before 1855, its introduction being uncertain. Of burnished gilt with silver beaded star, the plate has the regimental number within a crowned strap inscribed 'South Devon' which appears surrounded by a wreath of half laurel and half palm. The single battle honours 'Dominica' was authorised on 9 February 1808. *(Image courtesy of the late Charles Thomas)*

185 A detailed sketch from Military Insignia of Cornwall by D Endean Ivall and Charles Thomas of an other ranks' brass shoulder-belt plate. *(Image courtesy of the late Charles Thomas)*

47th (The Lancashire) Regiment

186 Here we have a rectangular gilt back plate which has mounted upon it a wide facetted star of eight points. On this is more silver in the form of the Royal Crest at the closure of a wreath which, at its base, has two battle honours on scrolls: 'Ava' and 'Tarifa'. Moving now inwards from the wreath, there are three more honours, 'Vitoria', 'Peninsular' and 'St Sebastian', then a strap inscribed 'Lancashire'. The regimental number is shown at the centre in Roman numerals. A Rose, an old badge of the 47th, has been placed just below the buckle of the strap. Turning now to Major Parkyn, we read that the same pattern had been worn in silver until replaced in 1830 by the silver and gilt version illustrated. *(Photo courtesy of The Military Campaign)*

187 An officers' gilt plate for the shako authorised by General Order 65 of June 1869. The Rose at the base of the Garter, the Red Rose of Lancaster, is an old badge of the 47th thought to have first appeared around 1818. *(Photo courtesy of Coldstream Military Antiques)*

48th (Northamptonshire) Regiment

188 An officers' shoulder-belt plate with silver mountings. Major Parkyn dates this item as having been in use between 1820 and 1855. *(Photo courtesy of Noble Numismatics)*

189 The other ranks' glengarry badge of 1874 to 1881. *(Photo courtesy of Regimental Badges)*

49th (or the Princess Charlotte of Wales's) (Hertfordshire) Regiment

190 Here we have an officers' shoulder-belt-plate. The regimental number appears in silver and has been placed in the centre of a crowned strap above a union wreath—eg shamrocks, a rose and thistle. The strap has been inscribed with the title 'Princess Charlotte of Wales's Regt.' Below the crowned circle the action that took place at Queenston Heights Upper Canada (now Ontario) on 13 October 1812 is remembered, the battle honour in the form of 'Queenstown' being authorised for the 49th on 27 January 1816. The Dragon of China is another battle honour awarded to the 49th, this time for its services in the China War of 1840 to 1842. *(Photo courtesy of Bosley's Military Auctions)*

191 A burnished gilt officers' plate with silver mounts of the number '49' and a Union wreath within a crowned strap inscribed 'Princess Charlotte of Wales's Regt'. To either side, and across the bottom of the plate, scrolls inscribed with the battle honours 'Copenhagen', 'Egmont Op Zee' and 'Queenstown'. An article in Volume XVIII (page 124) of the *Journal of the Society for Army Historical Research* dates this item as 1820 to 1842. *(Photo courtesy of the Military Campaign)*

192 In use during the period 1843 to 1855, this matted surface gilt plate displays a scroll inscribed 'Egmont Op Zee' on the left and another with 'Copenhagen' on the right. At the bottom two more scrolls, one with 'Queenstown', the other with 'China'. The latter, together with the Dragon displayed at the bottom of the plate, were awarded to the 49th for its services during the China War of 1840 to 1842. *(Photo courtesy of The Military Campaign)*

193 The other ranks' all brass plate worn on the Albert Shako of 1844 to 1855. The crown sits on a circle edged with a raised wreath of oak on the left side, and one of laurel on the right. The number appears on a lined background. *(Photo courtesy of Coldstream Military Antiques)*

50th (Queen's Own) Regiment

194 The 50th Regiment had been given the title of 'Queen's Own' in 1831. We can see it here on a crowned gilt strap at the centre of a fine officers' shoulder-belt plate. Within the strap, the silvered regimental number appears on a domed backing. The crowned strap has been placed upon a facetted silver eight-pointed star which extends almost to each of the item's four edges. Also in silver, and in recognition of the services of the regiment during the 1801 campaign in Egypt, the Sphinx upon a tablet inscribed with 'Egypt' which sits on the lowest point of the star. *(Photo courtesy of The Military Campaign)*

51st (2nd Yorkshire West Riding) Light Infantry Regiment

195 It was in 1809 that the then 51st (2nd Yorkshire West Riding) Regiment of Foot took on a light infantry role and the new title of '51st (2nd Yorkshire West Riding) Light Infantry.' The regimental number appears in the centre of what may be considered a standard-type bugle horn complete with ribbons. More familiar to this regiment (and its post-1881 successor, the King's Own Yorkshire Light Infantry), however, is the French-style instrument. Regarding the bugle horn, Major Parkyn explains how 'The date the design of a French bugle-horn was adopted by the 51st in place of the more ordinary one is not certain.' The author of the most valuable reference work, *(Military) Shoulder-Belt Plates and Buttons*, then goes on to recall how 'According to tradition, it was adopted by the 51st after the battle of Waterloo to commemorate the Regiment's engagement with a French regiment of Mounted Chasseurs whose badge it was.' Surrounding the bugle and number is a crowned wreath of laurel and below this, the motto Ich Dien (I serve). *(Photo courtesy of Coldstream Military Antiques)*

196 Following on from the previous shoulder-belt plate, this very fine officers' example features the French-style bugle horn. Set with the regimental number in the curl, it is shown among sprays of laurel interlaced with ornamental scrolls bearing the names of battle honours: 'Corunna', 'Salamanca', 'Orthes', 'Pyrenees', 'Minden', 'Nivelle', 'Peninsula', 'Waterloo' and 'Vittoria'. The whole includes a Guelphic, crimson backed, crown and is in silver upon a seeded gilt rectangular plate. *(Photo courtesy of The Military Campaign)*

197 An officers' plate for the shako introduced in 1861 and worn until 1869. *(Photo courtesy of Bosley's Military Antiques)*

198 A detailed watercolour painting by Richard Simkin featuring an officer wearing the Bell-topped shako of 1829 to 1844. The artist shows the shako plate in good detail: a gilt universal crowned star with a silver bugle and '51' in the centre. The shoulder-belt plate is that shown at illustration 195. *(Image courtesy of the Anne SK Brown Military Collection, Brown University Library)*

52nd (Oxfordshire Light Infantry) Regiment

199 This sketch from Almack's book shows an oblong shoulder-belt plate, silver and with the regimental number on a lined ground.

200 Photograph of a group of bandsmen who wear the number '52' with a bugle above in their round caps. The image has been marked with the date '1862'.

53rd (Shropshire) Regiment

201 The other ranks' brass plate for the shako authorised by General Order 65 of June 1869 and worn by infantry regiments until the introduction of the home service helmet in 1878. *(Photo courtesy of Coldstream Military Antiques)*

202 The other ranks' brass glengarry badge of 1874 to 1881. *(Photo courtesy of Coldstream Military Antiques)*

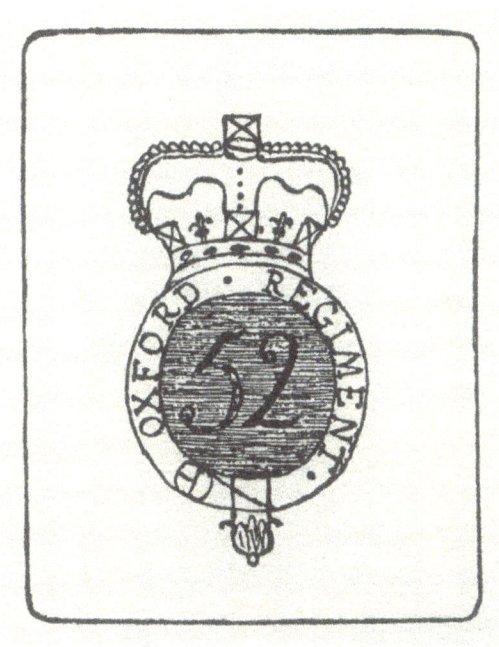

203 In this photograph of 'B' Company officers and sergeants taken during the early months of 1881, we see the number '53' worn at the front of a forage cap. Glengarries are also being worn, these having the badge illustrated at No 202. *(Photo courtesy of Alan Seymour)*

204 An interesting photograph showing the band of the 53rd, some of its members wearing the home service helmet with plates (see illustration 201) taken from the shakos previously in use. *(Photo courtesy of Alan Seymour)*

54th (West Norfolk) Regiment

205 A fine example of the officers' shako plate of 1861 to 1869. *(Photo courtesy of Coldstream Military Antiques)*

Officers & Sergeants - B Company 1st Kings Shropshire Lt Infty 1881.

Band 1st Kings Shropshire Lt Infty 1881.

55th (Westmoreland) Regiment

206 Sketch of an early oval shoulder-belt plate worn by officers. All in gilt, the regimental number appears within a crowned strap inscribed 'Westmoreland'. Surrounding this, some very fine, intricate engraving work.

207 Sketch of a matted gilt shoulder-belt plate with burnished edge. The figure of a dragon together with the word 'China', seen here within the centre of a strap, was awarded to the 55th on 12 January 1843.

56th (West Essex) Regiment

208 A scarce example of a Georgian officers' silver gilt shoulder-belt plate which Major Parkyn places as 'about 1790'. Engraved is the crowned Royal 'GR' Cypher which has 'Gibraltar'. The 56th had been involved at the defence of Gibraltar, 1779 to 1783. *(Photo courtesy of The Military Campaign)*

209 In this photograph of a group of senior NCOs, forage caps are seen which have the numeral '56' with the Gibraltar Castle above. Glengarry caps are also worn which have brass badges of the numeral '56' within a strap inscribed with the Gibraltar motto *'Montis insignia calpe'* (Badge of the rock of Gibraltar). Above the strap, the Castle and Key of Gibraltar with the arms of Essex (a shield charged with three seaxes) below the number.

57th (West Middlesex) Regiment

210 Formed in 1755, the original number of the 57th Regiment was 59th. It became the 57th in 1757, 57th (West Middlesex) Regiment in 1782 and 1st Battalion Duke of Cambridge's Own (Middlesex Regiment) in 1881. The 57th had fought bravely at the small Spanish village of Albuhera during the Peninsular War and the honour awarded for that action can be seen above the crown and number on the shoulder-belt plate illustrated. Major HG Parkyn includes a sketch of this item and states that it was worn by other ranks from around 1836 until 1855. The single honour 'Albuhera' would appear on many of the regiment's insignia, including its familiar post-1881 cap badge. *(Photo courtesy of Coldstream Military Antiques)*

211 A group of officers wearing forage caps with '57' at the front.

212 A fine example of the officers' plate worn on the shako of 1869 to 1878. *(Photo courtesy of Coldstream Military Antiques)*

58th (Rutlandshire) Regiment

213 Sketch from Almack's book of the gilt shoulder-belt plate worn c1800. Major Parkyn notes that this item was probably in use until around 1816.

59th (2nd Nottinghamshire) Regiment

214 Officers' rectangular shoulder-belt plate in burnished gilt with silver laurel wreath and separate crown. The regimental number 'LIX' appears in the centre above and arched, rope edged pierced scroll 'Bhurtpore'. Six other battle honours similarly displayed appear: 'Java', 'Peninsular' and 'Nive' at the top, and 'Vittoria', 'Corunna' and 'St Sebastian' at the bottom. *(Photo courtesy of Coldstream Military Antiques)*

215 Major Parkyn dates this magnificent Rocco-style officers' shoulder-belt plate in gilt, silver and red and blue enamels as 1846 to 1855. The regimental number 'LIX' appears on a blue ground in the centre of a red strap displaying the title, '2nd Nottingham'. The battle honour 'Java' has been placed above, and a further seven other honours, 'St Sebastian', 'Nive', 'Peninsula', Bhurtpore', 'Vittoria', Corunna' and 'Cape of Good Hope' appear on the elongated gilt rays of a silver star. *(Photo courtesy of Les Martin)*

216 The other ranks' brass glengarry badge of 1874 to 1881. *(Photo courtesy of Coldstream Military Antiques)*

60th (King's Royal Rifle Corps)

217 In this sketch from *The Annals of the King's Royal Rifle Corps* (Appendix) we have an officers' engraved silver shoulder-belt plate which has been dated as '1800 (or earlier)—1812'.

218 The other ranks' brass shoulder-belt plate of 1800. From *The Annals of the King's Royal Rifle Corps* (Appendix), this sketch shows the 'Royal Americans' and '60th' title in use after 1757. The regiment had been raised in New York and Philadelphia as 62nd (Royal Americans) in 1755.

219 The officers' silver shoulder-belt plate of 1812 to 1815 showing the Royal 'GR' cypher between a crown and regimental number. Sketch from *The Annals of the King's Royal Rifle Corps* (Appendix).

220 A final sketch from *The Annals of the King's Royal Rifle Corps* (Appendix) showing a bronze shako plate of 1830 to 1834. Battle honours fill the four arms of the cross, a further two appearing just above and below. The regiment's Maltese cross badge, according to its published history, was adopted from Hompesch's Regiment from which the 5th Battalion had been largely raised. The bugle had also originated from the 5th, and we can see it here in the centre with '60' within its strings. The title, 'The Duke of York's Own Rifle Corps', had been added in 1824 and remained as such until King William IV came to the throne in 1830.

61st (South Gloucestershire) Regiment

221 A superb example of an officers' plate from the stock of The Military Campaign which displays seven battle honours upon the points of a gilt crowned star. Reading clockwise they are: 'Orthes', 'Pyrenees', 'Toulouse', 'Nive', 'Nivelle', 'Salamanca' and 'Talavera'. A further honour, 'Peninsula', is shown on a scroll below the strap which is inscribed 'S. Gloucestershire' and displays the regimental number in its centre. And below this, a Sphinx over 'Egypt'. The plate was worn on the 'Albert' shako which was authorised by a Horse Guards Memorandum dated 4 December 1843. *(Photo courtesy of The Military Campaign)*

222 The plate for the shako authorised via Horse Guards Circular Memorandum dated 16 January 1855 and worn until 1861. *(Photo courtesy of Coldstream Military Antiques)*

223 The other ranks' glengarry badge for the period 1874 to 1881.

62nd (or Wiltshire) Regiment

224 A splendid starburst covers almost the entire surface area of the shoulder-belt plate illustrated. In its centre, the regimental number within a crowned strap inscribed 'Or Wiltshire' with, below and on a scroll, the battle honour 'Peninsula' which had been authorised on 26 May 1829. *(Photo courtesy of Coldstream Military Antiques)*

225 This magnificent example of an officers' shoulder-belt plate is from the remarkable stock of interesting and rare badges held by The Military Campaign. With a highly polished rectangular gilt backplate, it has mounted upon it a crowned cross pattée, the arms of which are hobnailed. The regimental number is in silver on a lined centre surrounded by a laurel wreath in gilt. The 'Peninsula' battle honour was authorised on 26 May 1829 and appears on the upper arm of the cross. *(Photo courtesy of The Military Campaign)*

63rd (West Suffolk) Regiment

226 A magnificent officers' shoulder-belt plate from the catalogue of Noble Numismatics in gilt, silver and green enamel. Just two battle honours are displayed on silver scrolls: 'Martinique' at the top, and 'Guadaloupe' at the bottom. The regimental number, 'LXIII' is in gilt on a ground of green enamel and appears in the centre of a crowned gilt wreath of laurels. *(Photo courtesy of Noble Numismatics)*

227 An officers' plate from the so-called 'Bell-topped' shako introduced in 1829 having been authorised by Horse Guards Circular Memorandum dated 22 December of the previous year. On a universal gilt crowned star back plate, a silver star upon which has been placed a circular wreath of laurels in gilt. Within this, the regimental number in gilt Roman numerals. *(Photo courtesy of Noble Numismatics)*

125

64th (2nd Staffordshire) Regiment

228 The other ranks' brass glengarry badge of 1874 to 1881. A crowned strap inscribed '2nd Staffordshire', a Stafford knot appears above the regimental number in the centre. *(Photo courtesy of Regimental Badges)*

65th (2nd Yorkshire North Riding) Regiment

229 A general pattern gilt shako plate worn by officers of the 65th Regiment. *(Photo courtesy of Blues Military Collectables)*

230 A fine and extremely scarce example of the gilt plate worn by officers of a grenadier company on the Albert Shako of 1844 to 1855. In the centre, a strap bearing the title '2nd York North Riding' and the flames of a grenade issuing from the top has been enclosed within sprays of laurel leaves on the left and palm leaves on the right. Above the strap is a scroll inscribed with the battle honour 'Arabia', and at the bottom another with the word 'India'. The latter, along with the Royal Tiger superimposed upon the lower ray of the star, was to commemorate the services of the 65th in India from 1796 to 1819. *(Photo courtesy of Coldstream Military Antiques)*

231 An officers' gilt plate with silver crown over 'India', the Royal Tiger, 'Arabia' and '65'. *(Photo courtesy of Noble Numismatics)*

232 The other ranks' glengarry badge of 1874 to 1881. *(Photo courtesy of Bosley's Military Auctions)*

66th (Berkshire) Regiment

233 Here we have a fine example of a shoulder-belt plate worn by an officer of the regiment. On the gilt rectangular backplate has been placed a silver star with twelve rays, ten of which bear the names of battle honours: 'Douro', 'Talavera', 'Albuhera' and 'Vittoria' appear on the upper rays, 'Nive', 'Pyrenees', 'Nivelle' and 'Orthes' on the lower. A ninth honour, that for the Peninsular campaign, has been split between the two central rays and appears as 'Penin' on the left, and 'Sula' on the right. The name of the regiment is shown on a crowned strap, in the centre of which has been placed its number in Roman numerals. *(Photo courtesy of The Military Campaign)*

234 A fine example of the officers' plate worn on the so-called 'Bell-topped' shako authorised via Horse Guards Memorandum of 18 February 1829. On a gilt universal crowned eight-pointed star a Maltese cross, the arms of which have the following battle honours inscribed: 'Talavera', 'Vittoria', 'Albuhera' and 'Nivelle'. Placed on the cross is a circle inscribed with four more: 'Orthes', 'Douro', 'Pyrenees' and 'Nive'. Within the circle on a silver ground, the numeral '66' within a wreath of laurel with below a ninth battle honour, 'Peninsula', all in gilt. The Bell-topped shako was replaced in 1844. *(Photo courtesy of The Military Campaign)*

235 From Bosley's Military Auctions, a superb example of the gilt plate worn by officers on the Albert shako of 1844 to 1855. The battle honour 'Douro' has been placed on a scroll just below the crown and 'Peninsular' at the base of the wreath. A further seven honours are shown on the main rays of the star: 'Talavera', 'Pyrenees', 'Nive', 'Orthes', 'Nivelle', 'Vittoria' and 'Albuhera'. *(Photo courtesy of Bosley's Military Antiques).*

236 The other ranks' brass glengarry badge, 1874 to 1881. *(Photo courtesy of Coldstream Military Antiques)*

67th (South Hampshire) Regiment

237 Major Parkyn notes that two oval shoulder-belt plates are recorded for the 67th. The first, a burnished gilt item, had just the regimental number engraved in the centre. For the second, reference is made to a miniature of an officer that appeared in the Autumn 1950 edition of the *Journal of the Society for Army Historical Research*. The subject established as a field officer of the last decade of the eighteenth century, the shoulder-belt plate being worn shows a crown with the number '67' below. In the original watercolour painting of a private in 1801 illustrated, artist KM Clayton includes a similar item.

68th (Durham Light Infantry) Regiment

238 Here we have an officers' silver and gilt plate from The Military Campaign which shows the regimental number displayed within the strings of a bugle. The battle honours 'Salamanca', 'Vittoria' and 'Pyrenees' have been placed on a three-part scroll above a crown at the top, with three more, 'Nivelle', 'Orthes' and 'Peninsula', appearing below a wreath at the bottom. *(Photo courtesy of The Military Campaign)*

239 In this original watercolour of an officer, signed and dated 1850 by Robert Richard Scanlan, the subject wears the shoulder-belt plate described in illustration 238. *(Image courtesy of the Anne SK Brown Military Collection, Brown University Library)*

240 An officers' plate from the shako introduced in 1869 and worn until 1878. *(Photo courtesy of Coldstream Military Antiques)*

68th (Durham Light Infantry) Regiment.

69th (South Lincolnshire) Regiment

241 This silver and gilt officers' shoulder-belt-plate displays four of the future 2nd Battalion Welsh Regiment's battle honours, 'Waterloo', India'. 'Java' and 'Bourbon'. They have been placed on tablets around a circle inscribed 'South Lincoln Regt' in the centre of which is placed the regiment's number in Roman, seeded, numerals. A laurel wreath moves up from just below the latter honour, terminating at the top just above 'Waterloo'. All this is mounted on a silver eight-pointed hobnail star. Major HG Parkyn dates this item as 1826-1855 and with the following comment: 'It is recorded that the plates were changed in 1826 before the regiment returned from India, just at a time when two new Honours, 'India' and 'Bourbon' had been given.' The 69th Regiment had received its 'South Lincolnshire' title in 1782. *(Photo courtesy of Coldstream Military Antiques)*

242 Photograph of a private, his cap bearing the metal numeral '69'.

243 The other ranks' shako plate for the period 1869 to 1878. *(Photo courtesy of Coldstream Military Antiques)*

244 The other ranks' helmet for the period 1878 to 1881. The numerals are separately attached.

135

70th (The Surrey) Regiment

245 The geographical designation 'Surrey' was added to the title of the 70th Regiment in 1782, but in 1812 the Prince Regent, in the name of his father King George III, had been pleased to change this to the 'Glasgow Lowland Regiment'. But a return was made to 'Surrey' in 1825. The name can be seen on a curved gilt scroll at the bottom of this superb officers' shoulder-belt-plate. Above this, and also in gilt, a crowned Garter with the number '70' in its centre. Both the crowned Garter and 'Surrey' scroll are placed on a silver eight-pointed star. *(Photo courtesy of The Military Campaign)*

246 In this unsigned watercolour study of a colour sergeant of the 70th Regiment, the plate worn on the shoulder-belt is that in use by the regiment c1840 to 1855—oblong with '70' in the centre of a crowned Garter with 'Surrey' on a scroll below on an eight-pointed star. The 70th was stationed at Barbados (Fort George to the right in the image) from January 1838 until June 1841. The headdress is the Bell-topped shako which has a brass crowned star plate with '70' in the centre. *(Image courtesy of the Anne SK Brown Military Collection, Brown University Library)*

247 An unusual plate, circa 1844-1855, from Bosley's Military Auctions with its cut silver Garter star on a gilt slip. Foliated, the regimental number appears in the centre of the Garter itself, which has a crown above and the word 'Surrey' below. The whole has been placed upon a rectangular seeded backplate. *(Photo courtesy of Bosley's Military Auctions)*

71st (Highland) (Light Infantry) Regiment

248 A French-style gilt bugle with the number '71' in the curl appears at the front of this company officers' shako of 1862 to 1881. Above this, a gilt thistle on a boss. A good representation from Player's Cigarettes.

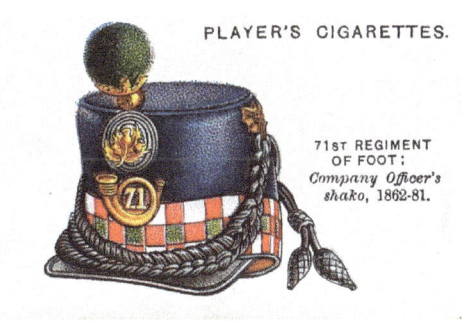

PLAYER'S CIGARETTES.

71ST REGIMENT OF FOOT: *Company Officer's shako, 1862-81.*

72nd (Duke of Albany's Own Highlanders)

249 The regimental title and number in silver have been placed on the gilt oblong back plate of this officers' shoulder-belt plate: '72' within a silver crowned thistle wreath, 'Duke of Albany's' on a scroll above. Two tablets, one inscribed 'Own', the other 'Highlanders' appear at the bottom. *(Photo courtesy of Coldstream Military Antiques)*

73rd (Perthshire) Regiment

250 A fine example of an officers' shoulder-belt plate in silver and gilt, in use by the regiment at 1855. Within a half-wreath, '73' appears between two battle honours, 'Mangalore' and 'Seringapatam', inscribed on roped-edged scrolls. Above this is a gilt crown, and below on a scroll, 'Waterloo'. *(Photo courtesy of Noble Numismatics)*

74th (Highlanders) Regiment

251 The badge of an Elephant had been authorised to the 74th for its services in India, and in particular at the battle of Assaye fought on 23 September 1803. Both the elephant and 'Assay' are seen here in the centre of this officers' silver plaid brooch which carries an 1866 hallmark and a manufacturer's name of JK Bearing of Edinburgh. *(Photo courtesy of Coldstream Military Antiques)*

75th (Stirlingshire) Regiment

252 In this coloured lithographic plate after André Léon Larue Mansion, the featured grenadier officer wears an oblong gilt plate with silver mounts of the Royal Tiger with crown and 'India' above. Below this is the regimental number in Roman numerals, 'LXXV', enclosed within a wreath.

76th Regiment

253 On this seeded gilt backplate has been placed a large silver device reminiscent of a Maltese cross with silver faceted rays between its arms. On the cross, and in bright gilt, is a crowned laurel wreath. Below the crown there are two honours, 'Hindoostan' and 'Nive', while below the wreath a scroll has the inscription 'Peninsula'. The 'Hindoostan' award was authorised on 20 October 1806 and to this honour was added the badge of an Elephant with Howdah in the following January. And here we see it, minus the howdah, above the regimental number 'LXXVI' in the centre of the wreath. *(Photo courtesy of The Military Campaign)*

254 An other ranks' example of the plate worn on the shako introduced in 1861 and worn until 1869. *(Photo courtesy of Bosley's Military Auctions)*

77th (East Middlesex) Regiment

255 A fine example of the officers' plate worn on the Albert shako of 1844 to 1855. Just below the crown is the Prince of Wales's Plumes, Coronet and motto Ich dien (I serve), and on four of the points of the star the following battle honours: at the top 'Seringapatam' and 'Ciudad Rodrigo', and at the bottom, 'Badajoz' and 'Peninsula'. The regimental number appears within a strap bearing the words 'East Middlesex'. *(Photo courtesy of Coldstream Military Antiques)*

256 The other ranks' all brass plate worn on the Albert Shako of 1844 to 1855. The crown sits on a circle edged with a raised wreath of oak on the left side, and one of laurel on the right. The number appears on a lined background. *(Photo courtesy of Coldstream Military Antiques)*

141

257 A pair of collar badges worn 1874 to 1881. *(Photo courtesy of Cultman Collectables)*

78th (Duke of Albany's Own Highlanders) Regiment

258 An officers' silver and gilt plaid brooch c1840 to 1848. The regimental number appears within a clump of thistles, and below this the motto *Cuidich'n rhi* (Help the king). *(Photo courtesy of Coldstream Military Antiques)*

79th (Queen's Own Cameron Highlanders) Regiment

259 In this gilt shoulder-belt-plate, the regimental number is displayed in Roman numerals within a crowned wreath. The design is mounted on a frosted surface and was worn, according to Major Parkyn, between 1840 and 1881. *(Photo courtesy of The Military Campaign)*

260 An officers' silver plaid brooch featuring the Sphinx over the regimental number in Roman numerals, 'LXXIX' and the battle honours 'Peninsular' and 'Waterloo' within a circular wreath of thistles. *(Photo courtesy of Coldstream Military Antiques)*

80th (Staffordshire Volunteers) Regiment

261 An article by the Rev P Sumner that appeared in the *Journal of the Society for Army Historical Research* (Vol XXI, Autumn 1942) dates this officers' shoulder-belt plate as '1816-17'. Rectangular in shape, it has silver mountings on gilt in the form of a crown above a Sphinx upon a tablet inscribed 'Egypt', the number '80' and a Stafford knot. The Sphinx was authorised on 6 July 1802 and commemorates the services of the 80th during the campaign of the previous year. *(Photo courtesy of Noble Numismatics)*

262 The brass other ranks' glengarry badge of 1874 to 1881, a crowned strap inscribed 'Staffordshire Volunteers' with in its centre a Stafford knot and regimental number. *(Photo courtesy of Coldstream Military Antiques)*

81st (Loyal Lincoln Volunteers) Regiment

263 The central device of this waist-belt clasp is from the arms of the City of Lincoln: on a silver shield, a red cross charged with a gold fleur-de-lis. The connection with the cathedral city falls back to the raising of the regiment by Major-General Albemarle Bertie, 9th Earl of Lindsey in 1793, almost entirely from volunteers from the Lincoln Militia.

82nd (Prince of Wales's Volunteers) Regiment

264 A fine example of the plate worn on the shako authorised by General Order 65 of June 1869. *(Photo courtesy of Coldstream Military Antiques)*

83rd (County of Dublin) Regiment

265 This rectangular gilt plate to the 83rd, later in 1881 1st Battalion Royal Irish Rifles, has sprays of laurel either side of a crowned collection of scrolls bearing battle honours: 'Talavera', 'Salamanca', 'Badajoz', 'Ciudad Rodrigo', 'Fuentes D'Onor', 'Toulouse', 'Busaco', 'Vittoria', 'Nivelle', 'Orthes' and 'Peninsula'. The regimental number appears on a domed centre. *(Photo courtesy of Coldstream Military Antiques)*

266 An other ranks' brass plate worn on the shako introduced in 1861 and in use until 1869. The plate is in one piece with the numbers cut out. *(Photo courtesy of Coldstream Military Antiques)*

267 The other ranks' brass glengarry badge of 1874 to 1881. *(Photo courtesy of Coldstream Military Antiques)*

84th (York and Lancaster) Regiment

268 An officers' oblong shoulder-belt plate with silver mounts of '84' and a Union Rose within a strap inscribed 'York & Lancaster'. The Rose had come with the title in 1809. Around the strap is a laurel wreath, and above that a crown over a scroll inscribed 'India'. Below the strap two more scrolls, one inscribed 'Nive' and the other 'Peninsular'. This plate, according to Major Parkyn, was the one in use in 1836. *(Photo courtesy of Bosley's Military Auctions)*

269 A fine example of the plate worn by officers on the 'Bell-topped' shako of 1829 to 1844. On a gilt universal star plate, a Maltese cross in silver which has battle honours displayed on three of its arms: 'India', 'Peninsular' and Nive'. In the centre of the cross, a gilt and silver rose with the regimental number '84'.

270 The officers' plate for the shako of 1869 to 1878, gilt with a silver rose mounted on the base of the wreath. *(Photo courtesy of Bosley's Military Auctions)*

85th (The King's Light Infantry) Regiment

271 In silver and gilt, a fine example of an officers' shoulder-belt plate. The 85th (Bucks Volunteers) had been raised in 1793, added 'Light Infantry' to its title in 1808 followed by 'The King's Light Infantry' thirteen years later in 1821. The 'Bucks Volunteers' part of the title was dropped in 1827 and the regiment was thereafter known as the 85th (The King's Light Infantry) Regiment. The plate illustrated shows a bugle and the number '85' in silver, and the post-1827 designation on a crowned strap. Below this in a taught ribbon with the single battle honour 'Peninsula' which had been authorised on 6 April 1815. *(Photo courtesy of The Military Campaign)*

86th (Royal County Down) Regiment

272 From the Anne SK Brown Military Collection, a detailed portrait of James Kenneth Douglas Mackenzie. The officer is shown with an Albert shako of 1844 to 1855 and a burnished gilt shoulder-belt plate with an Irish Harp and number '86' within its strings. Major Parkyn records this item as having been worn prior to 1855. *(Image courtesy of the Anne SK Brown Military Collection, Brown University Library)*

87th (or Royal Irish Fusiliers)

273 This fine shoulder-belt-plate, with its seeded gilt rectangular back plate and flaming gilt grenade, has been recorded as being in use between 1827 and 1855. On the ball of the grenade is a representation of the Eagle taken from the French 8th Regiment by Sergeant Patrick Masterson during the battle of Barrosa on 5 March 1811. It was as a result of the regiment's conduct at Barrosa that the Prince Regent authorised the use of his name within the title of the regiment. The 87th had become a fusilier regiment in 1827 and in 1881 provided the 1st Battalion of Princess Victoria's Royal Irish Fusiliers. *(Photo courtesy of The Military Campaign)*

274 Major Parkyn notes how there were several variations of the plate shown in illustration 273, one of which had a silver grenade instead of gilt. This version appears in the original watercolour painting by Richard Simkin illustrated. *(Image courtesy of the Anne SL Brown Military Collection, Brown University Library)*

87th Royal Irish Fusiliers 1832.

88th (Connaught Rangers) Regiment

275 Lieutenant-Colonel HFN Jourdain and Edward Fraser's history of the Connaught Rangers mentions an oval plate with the design of a harp above the number '88' as being worn in 1806. A damage plate with that description is illustrated with the addition of '2nd Battn' between the harp and number.

276 This superb officers' plate from The Military Campaign has a rectangular seeded gilt backplate with burnished edges. A silvered star has been mounted on this, eleven of its rays being inscribed with battle honours. Clockwise they read: 'Orthes', 'Ciudad Rodrigo', 'Nivelle', 'Busaco', 'Vittoria', 'Peninsula', 'Toulouse', 'Salamanca', 'Badajoz', 'Talavera' and 'Fuentes D'Onor'. Placed on the star, and in gilt, is a crowned wreath of shamrocks which encloses a circle pierced with the title 'Connaught Rangers'. Below the wreath the motto *Quis Separabit* (Who shall separate us?) and two further honours in the form of a Harp and the Sphinx over 'Egypt'. *(Photo courtesy of The Military Campaign)*

277 A page from Jourdain and Fraser's history of the Connaught Rangers showing shako and shoulder-belt plates for the period 1835 to 1840.

278 A page from Jourdain and Fraser's history of the Connaught Rangers showing shako plates for the period 1835 to 1878.

Shako Plate. 1822-1830.
Breastplate Star. 1830-1844.
Shako Star. 1835-1840.
Breastplate. 1817-1822.
Breastplate. 1830-1855.
88TH

Shako. Officer's. 1835-1840.
Shako Plate. Officer's. 1870-1878.
Shako Plate. Rank and File. 1870-1878.
Shako Plate. Battalion Private's. 1839-1855.
88TH

279 A page from Jourdain and Fraser's history of the Connaught Rangers showing glengarry, forage cap and collar badges for the period 1871 to 1881.

280 The other ranks' glengarry badge shown at the bottom of the page in illustration 279. *(Photo courtesy of The Military Campaign)*

89th (The Princess Victoria's) Regiment

281 An early shako plate consisting of a crowned universal star of eight points. Placed on this, another eight-pointed star in silver and on that a wreath of laurel surmounted by a Sphinx above a tablet inscribed with the name 'Egypt'. The regiment had served in Egypt during the campaign of 1801. Three more battle honours appear on a wide scroll below the wreath: 'Java', 'Niagara' and 'Ava'. The regimental number in gilt is shown against a domed silver ground. *(Photo courtesy of Noble Numismatics)*

282 The other ranks' glengarry badge, 1874 to 1881. *(Photo courtesy of Coldstream Military Antiques)*

90th (Perthshire Volunteers) (Light Infantry) Regiment

283 In this original watercolour painting by Richard Simkin, a private of the 90th is featured wearing the Bell-topped shako of 1820 to 1844. The crowned star universal plate shows the regimental number within a bugle. *(Image courtesy of the Anne SK Brown Military Collection, Brown University Library)*

91st (Princes Louise's Argyllshire) Highlanders

284 Worn between 1830 and 1864, this shoulder-belt plate is of burnished gilt with the mounts in silver. The pierced letters on the strap are on a green enamel ground.

92nd (Gordon Highlanders) Regiment

285 A well-polished example of an officers' rectangular gilt waist-belt clasp with silver fittings. Just below the 'Peninsular' battle honour is the figure of the Sphinx on a tablet inscribed 'Egypt' commemorating the services of the 92nd during the campaign of 1801. *(Photo courtesy of Cultman Collectables)*

93rd (Sutherland Highlanders) Regiment

286 Major Parkyn notes that this officers' shoulder-belt plate came into use about 1837. The silver mounts show a crowned circle engraved with the title 'Sutherland Highlanders' and with the regimental number in the centre. Around this is a half-wreath of thistles, and below a three-part scroll, 'Cape of Good Hope'.

94th Regiment

287 The officers' shoulder-belt plate worn prior to 1855. Photograph from Jourdain and Fraser's regimental history.

288 A shoulder-belt plate and three cap badges from Jourdain and Fraser's regimental history.

289 Lieutenant-Colonel HFN Jourdain and Edward Fraser's history of the Connaught Rangers date this shako plate as 1872 to 1878. *(Photo courtesy of Coldstream Military Antiques)*

BREASTPLATE
94TH
REGIMENT.

Cap Badge.
Grenadier Company.
Circa 1850.

Breastplate.
Officer's.
1814–1818.

Glengarry Badge.
Rank and File.
1873–1881.

Forage Cap Badge.
Officer's.
1874–1881.
94TH

95th (Derbyshire) Regiment

290 Other ranks' brass glengarry badge for the period 1874 to 1881. *(Photo courtesy of Coldstream Military Antiques)*

291 An officers' silver and gilt waist-belt clasp. *(Photo courtesy of Les Martin)*

292 An unusual and scarce item from Coldstream Military Antiques in the form of a gilt mess waiter's button manufactured by S Firmin & Sons of St Martin's Lane, London. *(Photo courtesy of Coldstream Military Antiques)*

96th Regiment

293 There had been several regiments with the number 96th. The plate illustrated, however, is that worn by the 96th raised in 1824. A frosted gilt plate, the star is in silver with a gilt crowned Garter with pierced motto. *(Photo courtesy of Noble Numismatics)*

97th (Earl of Ulster's) Regiment

294 The other ranks' glengarry badge of 1874 to 1881. *(Photo courtesy of Coldstream Military Antiques)*

99th (Duke of Edinburgh's) Regiment

296 This unusual pinned-back hallmarked silver item from Noble Numismatics comprises a belt bearing the raised letters 'Duke of Edinburghs Regiment' within which is the duke's coronet and cypher. The number '99' appears just above the buckle of the strap. The reverse of the item is shown, and this has been inscribed with what is possibly the name of its original owner, 'GG Blaxland 99th Regt.' George Glendower Blaxland had been commissioned as ensign in the 99th on 23 December 1864 and is shown in the Army List as Adjutant with a date of 28 May 1873. He does not appear after 1876. *(Photo courtesy of Noble Numismatics)*

98th (The Prince of Wales's) Regiment

295 Sketch from *(Military) Shoulder-Belt Plates and Buttons* of a gilt with silver star and gilt crown wreath and numerals. Raised in 1824, this seems to have been the only plate worn by officers of the regiment.

100th (Prince of Wales's Royal Canadian) Regiment

297 An officers' silver and gilt waist-belt clasp.

101st (Royal Bengal Fusiliers) Regiment

298 The other ranks' brass fur cap grenade.

102nd (Royal Madras Fusiliers) Regiment

299 The other ranks' glengarry badge of 1874 to 1881. *(Photo courtesy of Coldstream Military Antiques)*

300 The other ranks' fur cap grenade. *(Photo courtesy of Coldstream Military Antiques)*

103rd (Royal Bombay Fusiliers) Regiment

301 The other ranks' glengarry badge of 1874 to 1881. *(Photo courtesy of Coldstream Military Antiques)*

104th (Bengal Fusiliers) Regiment

302 The other ranks' brass glengarry badge, 1874 to 1881.

105th (Madras Light Infantry) Regiment

303 The other ranks' glengarry badge of 1874 to 1881. *(Photo courtesy of Coldstream Military Antiques)*

304 A fine example of the officers' home service helmet plate worn from 1878 until 1881. A special pattern, the Garter has been omitted from the universal crowned star. Within a laurel wreath there is a second smaller one made up of laurel (left) and palm (right). Across the base of this is a scroll inscribed *'Cede nullis'* (Yield to none), the motto of the former 2nd Madras Infantry which had been re-designated as the 105th Regiment when it joined the British Line in 1861. In the centre, and extending onto the wreath on either side, is a bugle inscribed 'Madras Light Infantry', and within the curl of the bugle is the numeral '105'. *(Photo courtesy of The Military Campaign)*

106th (Bombay Light Infantry) Regiment

305 The other ranks' glengarry badge of 1874 to 1881. *(Photo courtesy of Coldstream Military Antiques)*

107th (Bengal Infantry) Regiment

306 The other ranks' brass glengarry badge.

108th (Madras Infantry) Regiment

307 From The Military Campaign, a fine example of an officers' 1879-1881 helmet plate to the 108th Regiment. A universal crowned star, the plate has a double wreath. The regimental number in the centre is on a red cloth ground and the title 'Madras Infantry' is on a central strap. *(Photo courtesy of The Military Campaign)*

308 The other ranks' brass glengarry badge of 1874 to 1881.

109th (Bombay Infantry) Regiment

309 Officers' gilt button.

APPENDIX

(List of numbered regiments and their subsequent 1881 titles)

Pre-1881 numbers   **Post-1881 titles**

1st	1st and 2nd Battalions Royal Scots
2nd	1st and 2nd Battalions Royal West Surrey Regiment
3rd	1st and 2nd Battalions East Kent Regiment
4th	1st and 2nd Battalions Royal Lancaster Regiment
5th	1st and 2nd Battalions Northumberland Fusiliers
6th	1st and 2nd Battalions Royal Warwickshire Regiment
7th	1st and 2nd Battalions Royal Fusiliers
8th	1st and 2nd Battalions Liverpool Regiment
9th	1st and 2nd Battalions Norfolk Regiment
10th	1st and 2nd Battalions Lincolnshire Regiment
11th	1st and 2nd Battalions Devonshire Regiment
12th	1st and 2nd Battalions Suffolk Regiment
13th	1st and 2nd Battalions Somerset Light Infantry
14th	1st and 2nd Battalions West Yorkshire Regiment
15th	1st and 2nd Battalions East Yorkshire Regiment
16th	1st and 2nd Battalions Bedfordshire Regiment
17th	1st and 2nd Battalions Leicestershire Regiment
18th	1st and 2nd Battalions Royal Irish Regiment
19th	1st and 2nd Battalions Yorkshire Regiment
20th	1st and 2nd Battalions Lancashire Fusiliers
21st	1st and 2nd Battalions Royal Scots Fusiliers
22nd	1st and 2nd Battalions Cheshire Regiment
23rd	1st and 2nd Battalions Royal Welsh Fusiliers
24th	1st and 2nd Battalions South Wales Borderers
25th	1st and 2nd Battalions King's Own Borderers
26th	1st Battalion Cameronians
27th	1st Battalion Royal Inniskilling Fusiliers
28th	1st Battalion Gloucestershire Regiment

29th	1st Battalion Worcestershire Regiment
30th	1st Battalion East Lancashire Regiment
31st	1st Battalion East Surrey Regiment
32nd	1st Battalion Duke of Cornwall's Light Infantry
33rd	1st Battalion West Riding Regiment
34th	1st Battalion Border Regiment
35th	1st Battalion Royal Sussex Regiment
36th	2nd Battalion Worcestershire Regiment
37th	1st Battalion Hampshire Regiment
38th	1st Battalion South Staffordshire Regiment
39th	1st Battalion Dorsetshire Regiment
40th	1st Battalion South Lancashire Regiment
41st	1st Battalion Welsh Regiment
42nd	1st Battalion Black Watch
43rd	1st Battalion Oxfordshire Light Infantry
44th	1st Battalion Essex Regiment
45th	1st Battalion Derbyshire Regiment
46th	2nd Battalion Duke of Cornwall's Light Infantry
47th	1st Battalion North Lancashire Regiment
48th	1st Battalion Northamptonshire Regiment
49th	1st Battalion Royal Berkshire Regiment
50th	1st Battalion Royal West Kent Regiment
51st	1st Battalion Yorkshire Light Infantry
52nd	2nd Battalion Oxfordshire Light Infantry
53rd	1st Battalion Shropshire Light Infantry
54th	2nd Battalion Dorsetshire Regiment
55th	2nd Battalion Border Regiment
56th	2nd Battalion Essex Regiment
57th	1st Battalion Middlesex Regiment
58th	2nd Battalion Northamptonshire Regiment
59th	2nd Battalion East Lancashire Regiment
60th	King's Royal Rifle Corps
61st	2nd Battalion Gloucestershire Regiment
62nd	1st Battalion Wiltshire Regiment
63rd	1st Battalion Manchester Regiment
64th	1st Battalion North Staffordshire Regiment
65th	1st Battalion York and Lancaster Regiment
66th	2nd Battalion Royal Berkshire Regiment
67th	2nd Battalion Hampshire Regiment
68th	1st Battalion Durham Light Infantry
69th	2nd Battalion Welsh Regiment

70th	2nd Battalion East Surrey Regiment
71st	1st Battalion Highland Light Infantry
72nd	1st Battalion Seaforth Highlanders
73rd	2nd Battalion Black Watch
74th	2nd Battalion Highland Light Infantry
75th	1st Battalion Gordon Highlanders
76th	2nd Battalion West Riding Regiment
77th	2nd Battalion Middlesex Regiment
78th	2nd Battalion Seaforth Highlanders
79th	Cameron Highlanders
80th	2nd Battalion South Staffordshire Regiment
81st	2nd Battalion North Lancashire Regiment
82nd	2nd Battalion South Lancashire Regiment
83rd	1st Battalion Royal Irish Rifles
84th	2nd Battalion York and Lancaster Regiment
85th	2nd Battalion Shropshire Light Infantry
86th	2nd Battalion Royal Irish Rifles
87th	1st Battalion Royal Irish Fusiliers
88th	1st Battalion Connaught Rangers
89th	2nd Battalion Royal Irish Fusiliers
90th	2nd Battalion Cameronians
91st	1st Battalion Argyll and Sutherland Highlanders
92nd	2nd Battalion Gordon Highlanders
93rd	2nd Battalion Argyll and Sutherland Highlanders
94th	2nd Battalion Connaught Rangers
95th	2nd Battalion Derbyshire Regiment
96th	2nd Battalion Manchester Regiment
97th	2nd Battalion Royal West Kent Regiment
98th	2nd Battalion North Staffordshire Regiment
99th	2nd Battalion Wiltshire Regiment
100th	1st Battalion Leinster Regiment
101st	1st Battalion Royal Munster Fusiliers
102nd	1st Battalion Royal Dublin Fusiliers
103rd	2nd Battalion Royal Dublin Fusiliers
104th	2nd Battalion Royal Munster Fusiliers
105th	2nd Battalion Yorkshire Light Infantry
106th	2nd Battalion Durham Light Infantry
107th	2nd Battalion Royal Sussex Regiment
108th	2nd Battalion Royal Inniskilling Fusiliers
109th	2nd Battalion Leinster Regiment

BIBLIOGRAPHY

Almack, Edward, FSA, *Regimental Badges Worn in the British Army One Hundred Years Ago, Blades, East & Blades*, London, 1900.

Bennett, Major RW, *Badges of the Worcestershire Regiment*, RW Bennett, Bordon, 1994.

Ivall, DE and Charles Thomas, *Military Insignia of Cornwall*, Penwith Books, 1974.

Journal of the Society for Army Historical Research. Numerous issues consulted between 1821 and 2021.

Kipling, AL and King, HL, *Head-dress Badges of the British Army, Volume 1*, Frederick Muller Ltd, London, 1978.

Parkyn, Major HG, OBE, *(Military) Shoulder-Belt Plates and Buttons*, Gale & Polden, Aldershot, 1956.

Westlake, Ray, *A Guide to the British Army's Numbered Infantry Regiments of 1751-1881*, Naval & Military Press, Uckfield, 2018.

Westlake, Ray, *A Guide to the British Home Service Helmet 1878-1914*, Naval & Military Press, Uckfield, 2010.

In addition, more than 200 regimental histories have been consulted.

www.ingramcontent.com/pod-product-compliance
Lightning Source LLC
Chambersburg PA
CBHW061935290426
44113CB00025B/2924